C000108446

A Year in the Netherlands:
A Black Family in Europe

Lorene Kwapong

For information on bulk orders or other questions, please visit www.kakkwapong.com

To Mary and Napoleon Banks

ACKNOWLEDGMENTS

I like to thank the following people for their
support and motivation:
James Abraham, Cherri Banks, Patricia Jones, Lorraine Penn,
Dr. Alda Sainfort, Emmanuel Sainfort,
Sandra Sanders and Alonzo Dave Shelton.
Also, Kofi Kwapong, Ato Kwapong, Kwesi Kwapong, and
Vincent Kwapong for kindly allowing me to share their stories.

.

Contents

THE NETHERLANDS

NORTH SEA

SEA

Wadden Sea

GRONINGEN
Delfzijl
Ems
Groningen
Assen
Leeuwarden
FRIESLAND
DRENTHE
Heerenveen
Emmen

Den Helder

NORTH HOLLAND

IJsselmeer

FLEVO LAND

OVERIJSSEL
Zwolle
Almelo
Enschede

Alkmaar
Zaanstad
Markermeer
Lelystad
Haarlem
AMSTERDAM
Almere
Katwijk
Hilversum
Apeldoorn
Leiden
The Hague / 's-Gravenhage
Utrecht
Amersfoort
GELDERLAND
SOUTH
UTRECHT
Arnhem
IJssel
Delft
Lek
Nether Rhine
Rotterdam
HOLLAND
Merwede
Waal
Haringvliet
Dordrecht
Nijmegen
Rhine
Meuse
's-Hertogenbosch
Eastern Scheldt
NORTH
BRABANT
Breda
Tilburg
Flushing
Middelburg
ZEALAND
Western Scheldt
Eindhoven
Venlo
GERMANY
Antwerp
Scheldt
LIMBURG

BELGIUM

Meuse

Maastricht
Heerlen

Provincial capitals in red

A Wikipedia Map

March 2005: Spring Break Vacation

Vincent, my hard-working husband, had a job that kept him shuttling between the Netherlands and South Florida for about a year. He wanted to take us on vacation in the Netherlands for spring vacation. He treated us to a limousine ride to the airport. Kwesi, Ato, and Kofi, our three sons, loved eating the candy the limousine driver gave them.

Vincent had moved to Florida after graduating from business school to work for a multinational company in South Florida. Soon after that, most of the operations were moved out of the country. Vincent's projects had shifted to support operations in the Netherlands. This meant a lot of international travel away from us.

Looking back now I think Vincent was making our ride to the airport nice so that we wouldn't protest his larger plan—having us move to the Netherlands to join him. The flight was lovely and uneventful. The boys were entertained with hand-held games provided by the airline.

Amsterdam's Schiphol Airport looked like a museum. You could spend a day at the airport just looking at the fantastic artwork. As we were walking to pick up our luggage, the boys said, "That looks like Aunt Cherri." Surprise! It was Cherri, who had arrived two hours earlier from Pittsburgh and was waiting for us. Cherri is my oldest sister out of six siblings; three brothers and three sisters. She is single, without children, and a school board administrator. Vincent had secretly arranged for her to join us, yet another step in his plan to encourage us to make the major move to the Netherlands. We stayed in Amsterdam at the lovely and perfectly located Marriott Hotel. The hotel is directly across from the Rijksmuseum. The Rijksmuseum is home to all the Dutch Masters of art. The Marriott was pretty Americanized, as Vincent wanted to avoid culture shock. We stuck to what the boys knew; we ate downstairs at the Pizza Hut.

Cherri and I marveled at all the bike riders. This fascinated us, especially when we saw a sharp-dressed woman in stilettos stop her bike with her heels, then pedal on like no tomorrow. The weather was cold; we found out later that it is mostly cold and wet in March. We wore our winter coats. We took a ride on the famous canal sightseeing boat tour. It was an easy and relaxing way to view the unique architecture in Amsterdam—a must-do for first time visitors. We enjoyed ourselves on the calm canal water. The boys stood and tried to reach the tops of the tunnels with their fingertips as we passed under each bridge. Near the end of the trip, the calm canal opened up to a large body of rocky water, which took us by surprise. The boys were excited but sat down after being bounced around in the boat.

Amsterdam at night was elevated to another level. We faced the cold and ventured out at night and watched with awe the various street performers. The man eating fire held the boys' attention the longest. They walked into his performance circle and took pictures with him once he put out the fire.

* * *

A small-scale view of The Hague.

The next day Vincent drove us from Amsterdam to Den Haag (The Hague). The Hague is the capital of South Holland, the seat of the Dutch government and the home of Queen Beatrix. Our field trip was to Madurodam. We took a quick detour when Cherri spotted an outdoor market in Den Haag. The market was laid with cobblestone and had that old-world feel. Cherri and I jumped out of the car and into the light rain, looking at the stalls. Cherri bought jewelry to take back to the States as gifts. No one had an umbrella and the rain didn't seem to bother them. People kept chatting and shopping as if it was a warm and sunny day. Vincent and the boys waited in the car while we looked around at the stalls. Our boot heels kept getting stuck in the cobblestone street. We learned to tiptoe through the market.

Finally, we reached Madurodam, which means miniature city. We saw 1:25 scale models of famous buildings, airports, ships and other points of interest. The models were so real. The airplanes glided on the runway, windmills turned, a fire was being put out on a ship in a tiny recreation of the port of Rotterdam on the other side of

3

the park. The stadium was filled with tiny people watching a soccer match.

As we walked through the park, we began to feel like the giant in Gulliver's Travels. This was so much fun, the kids loved every minute. You can actually learn much about the Netherlands by reading the signs next to each exhibit and reading the booklet that explains each exhibit.

After a fun-filled day in Madurodam, we drove around the city of Den Haag. We looked at historic architecture and I wondered if this was The Hague that was mentioned on the news (it was). It took me a while to figure this out, but I got smarter the longer we visited. I soon could read some of the signs just by mentally subtracting the extra letters in a word and doing some rearranging of letters. The word noord, for example, is north.

We took pictures in front of the Peace Palace and the International Criminal Court, where war crimes trials are held. This information came from my well-informed, CNN-watching husband.

"Why do the boys always pose the same way when they get their picture taken?" Cherri asked.

"It's the Power Ranger stance," I replied. It's a boy thing, but we all posed as Power Rangers.

We drove to Rotterdam and saw the Euro Mast. The Euro Mast is a 186-meter tower. Kofi really wanted to go up. But it was cloudy and we voted not to go up the tower because we wouldn't get a clear view of the city.

* * *

The next day, Cherri and I broke away from Vincent and the boys and took our own field trip. We walked a few blocks to Albert Cuyp Market; this was more in her league. The market is named for a 17th century painter. It's a huge outdoor multicultural bazaar and has 300-plus stalls filled with everything from fresh flowers to fresh fish, from clothes to carpets and apples to zebra rugs. We were told we couldn't take the zebra rugs to the States but we could take them to other countries

Power Rangers take Amsterdam.

Imagine a super-sized farmers/flea market. You get the picture? It's a must do for shoppers. Cherri bought more jewelry for her gift collection.

I believed we walked past all 300-plus stalls filled with tourists and locals. We heard mostly local accents. Cherri and I shopped until my luck ran out and the cell phone rang. There was no escape. The boys wanted to know when we were coming back.

Later that evening we walked to the Vincent van Gogh Museum. It was a toss-up between the Museum and the Rijksmuseum. Van Gogh won out due to the dark painting displayed in front of the Rijksmuseum (it wasn't our style). On Friday nights, a lot went on there. We saw a live jazz band, watched a cooking demonstration, and looked at the great art of van Gogh. What amazed me most was that there are hundreds—it seemed like hundreds—of his paintings, other than the famous sunflower.

The paintings were organized into themes or years. For example, one room had his paintings from the period when van Gogh was using only dark colors, which was the way of the Dutch at that time. Another room had bright bold colors, the way the French painted during the late 19th century. It was easy to keep track of Vincent van Gogh's evolution as a painter. Not only were his paintings displayed, but also letters he wrote to his brother Theo and several artists. Again, I was so glad the Kwapong boys weren't with us; we would have been so distracted.

One of the biggest news a story was about the murder of Theodoor "Theo" van Gogh, the great-grandnephew of the painter. Theo van Gogh was a film director, film producer, columnist, and author with controversial views. He was killed after a film he made about violence against women in Islamic culture aired on Dutch TV.

We stopped at a gas station on the side of the highway and this is where we discovered how popular coffee is in the Netherlands. Even the local gas stations served better coffee than in the States.

Later in the week, we drove to Groningen. Vincent was scheduled to work while the rest of us continued with our spring break vacation. We stayed in the largest city closest to his job to make life easier for us to go sight-seeing, shopping, and finding entertainment for the boys. Vincent used the car to get to work. We had to find things to do within walking distance or depend on Vincent dropping us off and picking us up.

Groningen is the capital of the province of the same name. The University of Groningen is located here and gives the town a youthful and international vibe.

We stayed at the beautiful Schimmelpenninck Huys Hotel. This was our first Dutch hotel. It was similar to American hotels, except for the steep steps and a lot more hardwood. The bathrooms were smaller and we had a loft. There was an antique wooden spindle in the corner. The boys loved running up and down the ladder of the loft where their bedroom was located.

Vincent "discovered" the night life in Groningen. He took a walk and researched the "coffee shops." He explained to Cherri and me how the coffee shops operated. You can order various types of marijuana from a menu, just like you order coffee at Starbucks. But instead of just getting an expensive cup of coffee you get mind-altering substance and coffee. Vincent convinced us to go and see for ourselves.

He watched the boys while Cherri and I walked to the coffee shop, which, by the way, had a neon coffee shop sign in the window. The waiter/bartender explained all our options on the menu, as if we were ordering ice cream and wanted to know what the best-selling flavors were. He even told us the origin of the marijuana—"this is from Brazil," or "this marijuana is from Mexico." He could just as easily have been telling us that this "coffee is from Brazil and this coffee is from Mexico." We declined everything on the menu; we just wanted the experience of going to a coffee shop. We talked to the waiter/bartender about our lack of knowledge about the world of marijuana. We didn't order coffee, which they really did sell. Five dollars in the States gets you a cup of Starbucks coffee. Five euros in the Netherlands gets you a cup of coffee and fun. We guessed it was fun, but we didn't try it.

During breakfast the next morning we decided Vincent would drop us off in Roden, work half a day, and then come get us. Roden is 10 miles outside Groningen. Vincent dropped us off at Kinderwereld (Children's World Museum) and he went to work. Vincent told us he would pick us up in a few hours. Kinderwereld is a hands-on museum with wooden and antique toys that children can actually play with and ride on. A huge Ferris wheel and an Eiffel Tower made of K'Nex construction toys caught our attention first.

We watched trains go around villages as a hot air balloon floated in the sky. The boys made kaleidoscopes in the craft room. We pretended to be students in a traditional Dutch school room with old wooden instead of metal school desks and book satchels instead of backpacks. We wrote on wooden slates instead of typing on computers. But in another room we were quickly teleported to the future with computer games. We saw three Dutch boys sitting at the com-

Kofi and Kwesi enjoy Kinderwereld

puters. When we walked into the room they got off the computers and politely offered them to the boys to play games, The Kwapong boys quickly accepted. We were impressed by the Dutch boys' kindness.

Kinderwereld has a huge play area. Our favorite activities were riding around on the large tricycles and trying to walk, without luck, on wooden stilts. We enjoyed riding the old-fashioned merry-go-round and pulling each other in the wagons. We played carnival games and jumped rope, my favorite kid game.

Hours went by and Cherri said, "I thought Vincent was going to pick us up in a few hours. We got punk'd." We made the most of our time in Roden. We window-shopped, ate lunch, walked up and down the streets of Roden, and ran out of things to do since we didn't know where we were and this was our first time there.

We felt like we were on the MTV's television show "Punk'd," where a joke is played on someone. The joke ended six hours later when Vincent finally returned to pick us up.

After the long wait for Vincent, we drove another 35 minutes or so to another kid attraction. Speelstad Oranje (Playtown Orange) is

Ato, Kwesi, and Kofi looking for a McDonald's

located in Orange, Netherlands. It began to sprinkle, but it didn't matter because one of Speelstad Oranje's main attractions is an indoor roller coaster. Vincent went with the boys and rode the roller coaster while Cherri and I drank coffee. Kofi came back with a big smile on his face; Vincent did not look thrilled.

One day, we accidentally drove down the red-light district of Groningen. Not to be outdone by Amsterdam, Groningen has its own red-light district. Prostitutes dressed in lingerie and other skimpy outfits were standing or sitting in the display windows like live mannequins. Some women were shapely and some not so svelte. The boys never looked up from their Game Boys as we rode around. The red-light district was located in the same area as the regular stores. You literally turn the corner and bump right into a lady in the window next to a bakery.

Cherri's spring break was coming to a close and we did not want her to leave Amsterdam without visiting the Anne Frank House Museum. It was late and beginning to drizzle. Cherri and I again jumped out of the car and quickly toured the museum while Vincent drove around the block several times since it was impossible to find parking.

On the "road" at Verkeerspark.

Due to a glass addition to the original structure the building appeared modern. We read original writings of the Frank family and watched videos and film clips of the history of the Holocaust. There was a small room roped off that we could peep in but not walk inside. Most of the authentic house where Anne Frank actually hid was cut off to the public.

Our week was winding down fast. We moved from our hotel to Vincent's temporary apartment in downtown Groningen where he lived while he worked in the Netherlands. One day, Vincent dropped us off at Verkeerspark (Traffic Park for Children) in Assen while he went to work, which meant we had to stay all day. We were able to get along quite easily because everyone spoke Dutch and English.

The boys drove cars with pedals and stopped for gas at the Shell gas station. There was a huge castle where Kwesi played on the top level for a long time, shooting balls down at us. A Dutch boy was throwing the balls back, trying to hit Kwesi. Kofi was running through a maze of obstacles while Ato was walking on a wobbly rope bridge.

We had never seen so many bikes in one place until we visited Europe.

The playground had a big wooden tepee, a village of thatched huts, and a huge wooden airplane in which the boys played. What I like most about Verkeerspark is that you had to use your muscle power to make the cars move.

Later we went to the race car track and the boys drove a few laps; someone gave us free tickets. This was our first time eating kip nuggets (chicken nuggets), which became our favorite Dutch food with chips (fries).

After several hours the boys entertained themselves between playing in the indoor playground and the outdoor playground. I drank coffee and looked out the restaurant window as they played. This was the beginning of my coffee addiction.

I had another day of flying solo. Cherri had returned to the States and Vincent was always working; I had to find things to do on my own and within walking distance, so that we didn't depend on Vincent's work schedule. It was a clear cool day for walking to the nearby Groningen Museum. The Kwapong boys didn't like the museum, but I enjoyed myself.

Groningen Museum is a traditional museum (not a hands-on children's place) with beautiful glass vases, antique jewelry, and works of art by famous artists. The boys were impressed with the abstract shape of the museum and the fact that it sat in a canal and we walked across a bridge to get to it. In other words, with art you just look at it and say how pretty it is. The boys complained about the eight-minute walk from our apartment to the museum. They were not in a good mood, except for Kofi. He was happy because he was being pushed in a stroller.

However, they were more than willing to walk across the street to an impressive historic Dutch government building that is now a train station when they saw the Burger King sign hanging in the window.

The boys on the beach in Florida.

April 2005: We Are the Kwapongs

We are your typical family of five. Vincent works for Corporate America, (name withheld to protect the innocent). I am a stay-at-home mom and breast cancer survivor.

During our sojourn in Europe, Kwesi was 9 years old. He thinks inside the box. Ato was 7 years old. He thinks outside the box. Kofi was 5 years old. He thinks he is the box.

Vincent is from Ghana. I met him one Saturday afternoon while I was working at the Squirrel Hill Post Office in Pittsburgh. One of my duties was to lock the door at closing time. As I was locking the door I noticed a guy standing outside the door with a letter in his hand. He asked if he could mail his letter.

"Why didn't you get here before noon?" I asked.

"I ran all the way home to get the zip code," he said.

"Don't you know how to use the zip code directory?" I asked, feeling sorry for him. "Here, let me show you." I unlocked the door and welcomed him inside the lobby. The window clerks gave me the evil eye because they were rushing to close their drawers, count

their money, and go home. I walked him over to the zip code directory book and looked up the zip code for him. He wrote it on his letter and mailed it. I struck up a conversation with him. I asked him
where he was from and he said Boston. I laughed. I had never heard
a Boston accent like his.

One thing led to another, and I invited him to a party I had
planned for the evening. I drew him a map and wrote the directions
to my house. He came to the party and my friends thought he was a
nice guy. I told my friends I didn't know him, and joked that he
could poison the soup. Years later Vincent told me he gave his
roommate a copy of the map I drew and my phone number in case
he didn't return.

Vincent was then a student at Carnegie Mellon University. We
soon became friends. Vincent was a gentleman, whose habit of
opening car doors for me and reading what I read so that we could
discuss various topics was new and refreshing. After my friends
heard that he was from Ghana, they would ask questions such as
how many wives he had or was he a rich prince. Our friendship was
a comfortable one, until a fateful day.

"Do you want to watch me play soccer?" he asked. I said yes, and
he invited me to a game.

He took his shirt off; he was built like a god. The rest is history.
Those muscles won my heart.

Over the years, our marriage evolved into a long-distance affair.
We had three boys, but Vincent's studies and later business career
kept us apart for weeks at a time. So I learned to raise the boys
alone, with Vincent's occasional intervention when he was able to
come back home.

When Vincent quietly asked, "How would you like to live in Europe?" I automatically thought of Paris, Rome, or London. I think
Vincent used the word Europe to soften the blow. Then he said,
"Netherlands." Again, no news is good news, right? I didn't know
enough about the Netherlands to make a judgment. It wasn't on the
top ten things to learn in world history or geography class 20 years
or so ago. So I said yes. Kofi would be able to start school in grade
1. Kofi was in private kindergarten and in Florida his birth date

would have caused him to miss the cut-off to enter first grade with others his age.

We told the Kwapong boys that we were moving to Europe for one year. The boys agreed (as if they had a choice!). They said they could do it for one year only and after that they were moving back to Florida. The first things they wanted to pack were their Legos, PlayStation 2, and Game Boys.

We went on this adventure without a clue as to what to expect. Meanwhile, Vincent had been to the Netherlands many times before, but he didn't offer any help or suggestions. He didn't know the answers to the few questions I had.

Vincent was used to traveling. In Cambridge, Massachusetts, where he attended college, he had met a lot of people who had international backgrounds and were well-travelled. So he was open to the adventure.

Vincent said he wanted to give the boys a first-hand world view that would help them appreciate whatever society they found themselves living in. He told me once that he wanted us to live in Ghana or send our boys to an international boarding school. So this opportunity was a perfect piece to the puzzle.

Meanwhile, I conducted my own research. First, I asked my girlfriend, Amy, who had lived there.

"Everything is written in Dutch," she said. "I couldn't find an English newspaper or magazine. The Dutch children were bad, people rode bikes everywhere, and families shopped at the grocery store every day instead of loading up once a week at a supermarket. I was lonely. I was offended at first when I saw Sinterklaas [more on that later]. Plus, the weather was drab."

Amy lived in the Netherlands for three years and is married to a Dutch man. "At the time I lived in the Netherlands, I didn't like it. I didn't appreciate the Netherlands then, but I would now," she said. Strike one!

Next, I talked to Sally, a woman who taught at a community college in South Florida. Her husband worked for the same corporation that hired Vincent.

"I didn't like the Netherlands. It took me five years to get used to the weather. The Dutch are not friendly, and it was hard getting used to the lifestyle in the Netherlands. Your kids will be the only black people in school and the Europeans will want to touch their hair. They touched my kids' hair all the time because they are biracial."

Very interesting. Strike two!

Third, I called a friend from Pittsburgh named Big Dave. He's knowledgeable about these things.

"Be careful, you'll be staying close to the German border and may find some hostile racist people," he said. "Don't be surprised if someone tries to pick up you and Vincent in the Netherlands."

OK." Strike three!

Last, although technically I would have struck out by now, I found a fourth opinion. I told our long-time family friend, Lou, and his wife, Gwen, that we were moving to the Netherlands.

"I grew up in Groningen," Gwen said (who knew?). "I have cousins in the Netherlands. My grandparents are buried in Groningen. We're going to Paris and Amsterdam in the spring; we'll visit you."

Gwen's play of the day saved us in more ways than one.

We made the commitment with Corporate America, so there was no turning back. With all the advice and comments that people gave me, I still didn't know what to expect. I did know to pack the toys and not much of anything else. I couldn't think of what we would need. I wanted to keep clutter down. With three boys it wasn't easy. If I kept it simple, it would all work out.

Right?

What's public in Europe would not be public in the United States.

July 2005: Culture Shock

Vincent and I sent the boys to Pittsburgh with a friend, Marva, who was working in Miami for two weeks and flying back to Pittsburgh. The boys would stay with my family. How lucky could we get? I bought them Skittles and packed their Lego bag and off they went.

Marva said "I'll carry the Legos, if they drop the bag, Legos will spill everywhere and we'll miss our flight picking them up."

Vincent told Marva that we were moving to the Netherlands because Kofi could skip kindergarten, and when we got back Kofi would be in the 2nd grade. She laughed. I told Vincent not to tell anyone else that story. We would look really crazy if people thought we went to the Netherlands just so Kofi could skip a grade.

Vincent and I would be able to look for a new home and school, plus conduct any other business in the Netherlands without the boys harassing me. We flew to Amsterdam, rented a car, and drove to Groningen. Being without the boys was unusual and fun.

We ate dinner at a very expensive French restaurant. It was one of those romantic places where you're seldom sure if you're eating food or an artistic garnish.

When in doubt, I asked. This seemed to embarrass Vincent a bit.

"Everything is edible on the plate," the assistant chef said, even the tiny speckled boiled eggs, which Vincent advised me were pigeon eggs. Somewhere around the third course, we noticed two Dutch men sitting across from us enjoying their dinner with a bottle of wine. They smiled at us and we smiled back. After a while, one started to carry a conversation with us.

He asked, "Where are you from?"

"The States."

"Bush Country, you're from Bush Country, yeah?"

"We're from Florida, really Bush Country."

"Bush Country twice?" he asked. "Governor and president. What are you doing here, are you on business?"

"Yeah, I'm here on business," Vincent said.

"Are you here to cut a deal and then you'll leave, yeah?"

"No, I'll be here for a while," Vincent said.

"You look like a male version of Venus Williams, the tennis player," the man said. Now he was getting sort of personal. "You watch tennis?"

Vincent said, "Yeah, I watch tennis."

The man's friend was trying to get him to keep quiet and go back to their table, but it didn't work. He kept talking.

"What do you do when he is at work?" he asked. "Can I take you shopping while he's at work?

"No, thank you," I said.

"Are you sure? You need someone to show you around."

"No thanks."

Dave had warned us. I wasn't sure if he was trying to pick me up, or Vincent, or both of us. He talked to Vincent for a while and then he turned and talked to me. He gave Vincent the compliment, not me. I guess it was Vincent's muscles. I don't blame him, Vincent is one sexy man.

I also noticed how close the Dutch man was to us. We felt cornered. In the States we need our personal space. What's the rule? Keep an arm's length away. I later learned that Dutch people talk close and it didn't bother us after that.

After dinner, the chef came out to see if our dinner was satisfactory. In Europe, the chef comes out to see if you have any questions, explain how it was prepared and if you enjoyed their meal. Of course we did!

One evening in the hotel lobby at the Mercure Hotel (we changed hotels every other day, don't ask why), Vincent and I were having cocktails at the bar. The bartender struck up a conversation.

"Where are you from?"

"The States."

"How do you like it here?"

"We like it here," Vincent said.

"Have you been to the live sex shows?" he asked.

We both said no. I asked what they were like.

"They're a lot of fun," he said. "Sometimes my friends and I get dressed up or wear costumes and watch the sex shows."

"What is there for women to do?" I asked. "Can a woman get a man?"

"You could get a man, sure," the bartender said, warming to the subject. "Sometimes my girlfriends get together and get a man for the night, it costs about 100 euros. But a big black man like him (he pointed to Vincent), he could get about 200 euros a night."

I told you Vincent was sexy. And, as you can see, the Dutch are straightforward. I teased Vincent the rest of the year. I told him he could work on the weekends when we run low on euros.

Later during the week Vincent had an appointment with a consultant. The meeting took place in a conference room at the beautiful Golden Tulip Hotel. We met the facilitator. Vincent asked her if he could keep his computer on while she talked. She said, "No, turn off your computer." Vincent cannot live too long without a computer. A computer to Vincent is like air to most people.

Vincent tried to multi-task, but she didn't allow it. We spent the day learning all about the Netherlands. She answered all our questions about the Netherlands. We learned about history, political and social issues, the education system, manners, and etiquette. We even talked about sports. We left with a binder full of information to take to Assen, our new hometown.

Assen is a small quiet town with an odd combination of city and country life about 30 minutes from Groningen. It reminds me a lot of north Sarasota, where we now live. Vincent went to work, while I searched for a home and school with the assistance of Connect International. They're in the business of making life abroad easy for expatriates. The key word here is "business."

The search for the perfect house was quickly dismissed. I was told there are few homes for rent and most people live in apartments or rent their homes for years. I looked at about seven homes as Vincent pressured me to make a decision. My only requirement was a home close to the school. I chose a contemporary-styled medium-sized home.

Houses in the Netherlands are smaller and they usually have one bathroom. Our house had four bedrooms, two bathrooms and was supposed to be close to the school. I found out after we moved in that it wasn't close at all. I was used to living four blocks from our elementary school in Florida, even though I drove the four blocks. It was always too hot to walk.

I looked at a typical Dutch house with the steep stairs and ruled it out because of the stairs. I thought Kofi would fall down the steps. We went to this very same house for a play date about a month later and Kofi loved this house; he ran up and down the steps with no problem.

I realized after about a month or two I should have chosen a bigger house and one closer to school, but I couldn't make a clear decision in such a short time. I also found out later from talking to other expatriates that there were more homes to rent. They were also told that there weren't many housing options. Every time I visited a new friend their home was spacious and it would have suited our needs better. What I did love about my house was the kitchen. I don't cook much, but that was beside the point. It seemed all the Europeans have high-tech, sleek kitchens. We even had a built-in stainless steel appliance just for steaming. The sinks and bathtub were contemporary in design. This house was extremely clean, white, and sterile. I wondered if I could keep it as clean with three boys and maintain its museum-like quality.

In the Netherlands, TV is not the big deal it is in the States. We had one TV instead of one in every room, and took turns watching programs. This wasn't difficult because there were only a few programs in English. One was "Fresh Prince of Bel Air," the boys' favorite program. I watched "Desperate Housewives," "Oprah," "Dr. Phil" and CNN. There were a few really good British programs I enjoyed watching. The boys would watch cartoons in Dutch. Because they had seen them in the States, they already knew what was happening.

All the Dutch homes had wonderful gardens, including ours, which looked like something out of a magazine. I learned gardening from my mom in Pittsburgh. Her garden was really nice, plus she grew collard greens in between her flowers. The owners were an unmarried couple living in England. Couples living together without a marriage certificate were no big deal in the Netherlands. The owners left us a big binder of do's and don'ts. Inside the binder was the manual for every appliance in the house and who to call for repairs when needed.

The owners of the house gave me strict orders not to let the boys jump on the decorative rocks in front of the house and not to burn the stone counter top. Actually, there were too many orders. I was only to use certain pre-approved products for certain cleaning jobs. My Dutch neighbor quickly told me that I didn't have to follow all those rules.

I had a tour of both a British school and a Dutch school. An American family that had lived in the Netherlands for a year put their children in an international school and was not happy with the results. The mother felt that her children would have to repeat grades because they didn't learn anything during their first year in the Netherlands. She recommended the British School.

Gerta, my Dutch neighbor, was a teacher at the international school and she also recommended the British School. She said the Dutch children would beat up the Kwapong boys. The Dutch children play rough.

Gerta also helped me with our medical needs. She gave me the address of a doctor in downtown Assen. Normally, your doctor lives in the same neighborhood so that you could have medical care around the clock if needed. But the doctor in my neighborhood had just retired.

Then we returned to Pittsburgh to pick up the boys. Of all the things Connect International stressed, the most important item one had to have at all times was an apostille. We would not be able to stay in the Netherlands unless we had them. An apostille is a document that you have to get in person from the Secretary of the Commonwealth of your state. Our original birth certificates and marriage license weren't good enough. The world, according to Vincent, said we didn't need it. But I wasn't going to fly to the Netherlands with three boys and find out that we had to go back to Florida because I didn't follow directions. I only had a few days to figure out how I was going to get to Harrisburg and back in a day. Luckily, Carl, my nephew, was visiting from Ohio. Luckily, my brother, Lee, loaned me his car. Carl and I drove to Harrisburg and got the apostilles. An apostille is a gold state seal on a sheet of paper that authenticates a person's country of origin and birth certificate.

Each birth certificate has its own apostille. It took all of five minutes. We ate lunch and drove back to Pittsburgh the same day. That was the most stressful day of my preparations to leave.

August 2005: Belgium, Denmark, and Germany

Our first trip from the Netherlands to another country was to Belgium. The Connect International office gave us some suggestions on where to go and Belgium was recommended as a quick getaway. So one weekend, we just packed our bags and left. The journey to Belgium was an uneventful three-hour car drive from Assen going south.

Arriving in Brussels, we had a hard time finding our hotel. From the outside, it looked like a regular building in a dark alley. Once inside, the Hotel Silken Berlaymont opened up into a fantastic hotel with a stunning interior. The art was remarkable. The restaurant was stylish and the food good, even though the boys stuck to cheeseburgers. The staff was friendly.

The next morning we took a ride through a local neighborhood. Brussels looked very much like the cities in the Netherlands.

Miniatures everywhere!

I learned that Belgium was once part of the Netherlands. The language was similar. One of the hotel personnel told us he spoke four languages (French, English, Dutch, and Flemish). He said it is common that they speak three or four languages because Belgium sits between France and the Netherlands.

Our field trip for that day was to Mini-Europe in Brussels. We knew the boys would enjoy themselves. Mini-Europe is a park with mini-models detailed to a scale of 1:25 of famous buildings, technologies and points of interest in European countries. We saw a miniature Eiffel Tower representing France. We learned so much about other countries during this field trip alone. It felt refreshing to see something different, other than the usual amusement parks in the States with roller coasters and rides.

I haven't seen a miniature city in the States, but then, I haven't visited all fifty states. We were beginning to see a pattern with the miniature buildings, first in Madurodam and now with Mini-Europe.

Brussels is nicknamed the capital of Europe and is home to NATO. Our hotel was near a curved glass building that was being renovated. A few days later while we were watching the news we found out that this was the Berlaymont Building, which is the headquarters of the European Union. Many of the buildings in Europe are either historic or high tech. We took a different route home and enjoyed the scenes along the way.

* * *

Our next road trip was to Denmark, a long and boring six-hour drive on a flat stretch of land. Denmark is comprised of about 400 islands; the part that is actually connected to the rest of Europe is called the Jutland Peninsula. We left early, about five o'clock.

We used a McDonald's drive-through, and found out that once you crossed the Netherlands border you are on your own as far as English-speaking people are concerned. Fortunately for us, there was one waiter that spoke enough English to help us order our breakfast. The waiter at McDonald's gave the boys extra candy.

Along the autobahn, Germany's motorway, were signs with tourist attractions and famous places to visit. Vincent asked me if I wanted to stop, but I couldn't read the signs in time because he was driving so fast. By the time I read the sign and said, "Let's stop at..." we had already passed the exit for the attraction.

Vincent took full advantage of this speed-zone-free country. He was teaching me how to drive a stick shift. I bravely took the wheel. I didn't want to drive like I was crazy, but in Germany, you will get run off the road if you don't drive like you're crazy. I looked in the rearview mirror and I wouldn't see a car, then a second later I looked in the rearview mirror again and there was a car on my tail with bright headlights on for safety. I didn't know where it came from.

The only exciting part of the drive was when we drove past a shipping port in Hamburg, Germany. The boys fell asleep in the car and woke up a bit later and began complaining: "Why can't Daddy drive? Mommy drives too slow, she doesn't know how to drive. We're still in Germany," and on and on and on.

25

Vincent took over the wheel. Once on the Denmark freeway, there wasn't anything to see but the open flat road and a few bushes on the side.

It was very interesting to cross borders. The flag changed at the border and sometimes there were guards. For some reason this was exciting to us. Gerta, my Dutch neighbor, said it's just like crossing from state to state. But it's not the same at all. First of all, each country had a different language and the currency may or may not have been euros. The culture and customs were definitely different.

The capital of Denmark is Copenhagen. We knew we were a long way from home when the letters "a" and "e" looked backwards or they looked stuck together like the typed letters do when you type too fast. The word Copenhagen is spelled with a K. We couldn't make out any of the signs. I told Vincent, "We're not in Kansas anymore." The money was not euros, the currency was Danish krone.

The original LEGO-LAND opened in 1968 by the Lego Company. Ole Kirk Christiansen invented Legos in 1934. The name is from the Danish words "Leg Godt" which means "play well."

The language was not English, it was Danish. Whatever it was, we didn't have any. Good for us they took euros and credit cards to get into LEGOLAND. We had yet to do research about a country before a road trip.

It was a cloudy weekend and it looked like it would rain any minute. I suggested we go to LEGOLAND rather than wait. A day in Europe can look cloudy and it does not rain, or it can look cloudy and rain all day.

Once inside Legoland we saw large attractions of cities, airplanes, a dog, ships that sail in water, all built with Legos. It was quite amazing.

We didn't know what to look at first. We were all pointing at different things. I enjoyed the greenery, the plants and flowers were beautiful. I was so amazed that the plants were so vibrant with so little sun.

We enjoy a view of the miniature Eiffel Tower in Mini-Europe.

Kwesi took mental notes of the Legos so that when we got back to Assen he could duplicate what he saw. I told him to take pictures. We loved the Lego dog best of all. Kofi wanted to ride a roller coaster, but Vincent and I were scared.

I volunteered to go with Kofi and Ato on this roller coaster ride after the Lego employee assured me that it was nothing. It was fun, we did it twice. After a day of rides, the boys got to shop in the Lego store. They could not decide what to buy. We gave them a monetary limit. They ended up buying Lego men.

We walked to the parking lot and got stuck there because we didn't have Denmark money and no one around us spoke English. We waited about five minutes and a person appeared who spoke English and gave us kroners. Using this currency was the only way we got out of the parking lot. We were stared at a lot during our trip, but it didn't feel racist in nature as it does in the United States. It was more of a curiosity stare, almost like we were celebrities—well, maybe more like retired celebrities.

A fascinating city in miniature at LEGOLAND.

I believe we were the only black folks in sight for the next two days. We drove through the town of Billund, the home of LEGO-LAND, to our hotel in a lovely country town called Gadbjerg.

I wanted to stay at an authentic European hotel. We stayed at Hotel Margrethe. It's a quaint and old-fashioned looking building. Our breakfast was very Danish (I guess). The boys ate soft-boiled eggs for the first time.

They cracked their eggs in those little dainty egg cups. If I would have told them to eat a soft-boiled egg out of a cup in Florida, they would have cried. We also ate cucumber and tomatoes with our breakfast. After breakfast we walked around the neighborhood and took pictures. The architecture was more Swedish in design. We drove back early so that we could make a stop along the way home.

On our way back from Denmark we stopped in Hamburg, Germany. The port of Hamburg is the second largest container port in Europe and ninth in the world. It was amazing. Vincent was good at finding alternative routes without actually telling us we were lost.

A panoramic view of the Hagenbeck Zoo.

Vincent used his trusty GPS. We arrived in Hamburg not know-ing what to do. We stopped in the lobby of a hotel and grabbed a few brochures. I suggested that we go to the zoo. It turned out that we were only a few blocks from the Tierpark Hagenbeck Zoo. I knew from past experience that it is best to do children's activities to keep the peace.

Tierpark Hagenbeck was founded by Carl Hagenbeck, Jr., in 1848. He was the first to introduce moated animal exhibits instead of gated. It was very crowded for a zoo. I met an American woman and she said that the zoos were popular on Sundays. We walked through the Asian garden. There was beautiful Asian architecture throughout the zoo. We watched people feed the elephants out of their hands, only separated by a small fence. Why? We don't know. The elephants were bigger and stronger than the fence. We climbed inside a huge rock and at the top it overlooked the entire zoo. The weather was holding up. The boys ate cotton candy that was so white and fluffy it didn't look real.

We walked through the entire zoo. Vincent is big on maps, logic, and order. We followed the zoo map and covered the entire park in order, starting with number one, all the way to the last exhibit. At different times, we watched people holding their children over the edge of the lion's den or some other dangerous animal den. It was common to see kids dangling from their parent's arms. No one looked twice, but us. I'm sure Europeans didn't understand what the big deal was when Michael Jackson held his baby over the rail while in Europe.

I haven't noticed this practice at American zoos. We spent about three or four hours at the zoo and headed home to Assen. This turned out to be a good plan. We ordered McDonald's and, thank goodness, there was a teenage boy waiter who was eager to practice his English. He helped us order our food. We ate in the car to save time and everyone was happy.

September 2005: School, Home and Woods, Oh My!

School began on September 6. The Kwapong boys were dressed in their official school uniforms, white polo shirts with the school lion logo along with the standard navy blue pants. The boys attended the Helen Sharman School in Assen, which was part of the British International School in the Netherlands. Helen Sharman, the first British astronaut in space, visited the school every two years or so.

Kofi was in Year 1 (kindergarten), Ato was in Year 3 (2nd grade) and Kwesi was in Year 6 (5th grade). Kwesi's class was combined with Year 5 due to the small amount of students in each class. His class was referred to as Year 5/6.

I went to a THRASS (Teaching Handwriting Reading and Spelling Skills) demonstration at school for Year 3. Ato answered every question. His teacher said it was the Ato show. Ato even answered a question before his teacher asked the question and he got it right. Ato is truly gifted.

This reading system taught Kofi how to read surprisingly quickly even though Kofi claimed he could read a book without opening the book. How is this possible?

Kwesi went on his first field trip to BSN Vlaskamp in The Hague to visit the main British School for a sports event. He traveled by train and he stayed overnight with a family whose child goes to the British School in The Hague.

Kwesi was paired with Donnie, a boy from Florida; his father was a colleague of Vincent. Their activities included soccer, rugby, and instant Scottish dancing. Several parents were angry at the head teacher (principal) because they did not want their child to stay overnight with parents they did not know.

I was a happy parent, and packed Kwesi's clothes and lunch so fast. Sink or swim, that's my motto.

The majority of families attending the school worked for the Royal Dutch Shell Company located in Assen. We know it simply as Shell Corporation. The advantages and disadvantages were one and the same. We were not part of the gossip and therefore out of the information loop. One family lived about 10 minutes by car from our Florida home. I didn't know them when we lived in Florida. Americans become real friendly with other Americans when living on foreign soil.

I thought we could live with one car, but soon found out that it wasn't possible because the distance from the school was farther than I anticipated. The one requirement I had was to live near our school. I was told by Connect International that our house was a 10-minute bike ride away. In reality, it was more like a 25-minute bike ride.

So we had a bit of a rough start. I did not know how to drive a stick shift except on the highway. Vincent would drop us off at school in the mornings and go to work. After the boys were settled in their classrooms I would walk home. It took 40 minutes, and then I had to return to school by foot in the afternoon to pick up the boys. It took another 10 minutes to round up the three boys once school let out, as they would be off in different directions somewhere playing on the playground.

Donnie's mother, Sharon, offered to take us home. This was good, but we couldn't ask her every day. Then we tried a taxi service. Sometimes they would pick up the boys and other times I would get a call from school saying the taxi didn't pick them up. We tried biking, but Ato was too tired after school. I would put Ato on the back of my bike and Kwesi would take Kofi on the back of his bike. We had too many backpacks. The weather suddenly changed into cool and rainy. The route consisted of going through the busy town center, and three small black boys travelling alone on bikes in a foreign country was not my idea of fun. Even though the bike routes are very clear, it wasn't straightforward for kids.

Vincent thought they could ride by themselves and get toughened up in the process. "Let's give them a different lesson to toughen them up." I said.

I would practice driving around our neighborhood but couldn't see the light at the end of the tunnel. When Vincent tried to teach me we would make very little progress. Every time I asked Vincent a question he would say, "Listen for when the gears change." The gears made the same sound after every gear change.

Sometimes Vincent would give me different answers to the same questions. One night I slowly drove around our quiet neighborhood alone until it made some sense. After many weeks of struggle and the neighbors watching from their porches, I finally learned and we got a second car.

Our new home was four houses away from the woods. Nature is considered part of your total well-being in the Netherlands, but we were from the States. I talked the boys into walking in the woods. We carried sticks and made a game out of it. I didn't tell them I was scared to walk in the woods. I might run into a dog. The dogs were well trained, but still you never knew. But I didn't let my fear show in front of the boys.

The woodlands were only a five-minute-long walk before you reached a highway. The woods were divided by the highway then you were back into the woodlands for another five minutes. There were houses and shops at the end. I felt like the blind girl in the movie "The Village" by M. Night Shyamalan. When she walked to the edge of the woods, she was scared; and when she got to the edge there is a town full of people. Like the girl, we were close to people yet we panicked in the woods.

Kwesi was even scared of slugs on the ground. He wouldn't walk in the woods or outside the house if the slugs were out. Whenever Kwesi made his younger brothers angry, they would sing, "Kwesi's scared of a slug."

Woods aside, we found more pleasant nature encounters to occupy us. For example, the Ecodrome in Zwolle is a natural zoo/museum built inside a huge glass building. We were fascinated watching a very large aquarium filled with piranhas at feeding time. We also watched the beavers or otters at feeding time but they weren't as exciting—or dangerous. We played at an outdoor playground, paddled on boats, and ended our day eating kip nuggets at the restaurant.

* * *

We went to our scheduled interview at the government office Immigratie-en Haturalisatiedienst (IND) Immigration and Naturalisation Service to have our official papers documented for our year's stay in the Netherlands. While we had our interview, the boys played games; even in the government office there is a place for kids to play. Since everything was written in Dutch and conducted in Dutch we could not have completed this task without the help of Connect International. We had valid passports, additional color passport photos each, employment contract, permission to work in the Netherlands, proof of health insurance and, last but not least, the apostilles.

October 2005: Four Countries in Four Days—Germany, Switzerland, Italy and Austria

The school officials sent a letter home with the boys that explained the school's policy on unauthorized absences. It stated that absences for family trips or extended holidays were strongly discouraged and should be avoided. Attendance on the first and last day of each term is required. The Leerplicht Ambtenaar (Office of School Attendance) in the Netherlands regarded such absences as illegal and parents were subject to litigation. The letter even stated that the excuses must be in advance, supported by the family employer, and absences without permission could result in legal penalties. In other words, the Netherlands don't play.

The boys soon had a few days off for half-term break. Vincent was off Thursday and Friday, so he suggested a road trip. I wanted a plan of some sort and since we didn't have one, I would have been happy to have stayed home for the week. I told Vincent we couldn't keep traveling around like gypsies (no offense to gypsies).

I told Vincent we should see the places we really wanted to see first and as soon as possible. We never knew when Corporate America would change the plans and send us back to Florida without getting a chance to see Europe.

I packed our clothes for our road trip. Vincent told me to pack light—right. With three boys that was almost impossible, but I completed the task. The original so-called plan was to go to Switzerland. Vincent said it was a 4-hour drive to Frankfurt, Germany. The boys packed up two big bags of Legos and their Game Boys. I packed some snacks.

By 4 p.m. we were off into the unknown, without a map or information about Switzerland. We crossed over into Germany without a border patrol on guard. Six hours later we reached Frankfurt, Germany, at about 10 p.m. Frankfurt is metropolitan, with skyscrapers and modern buildings, even though the city is 1,300 years old. It's the financial, publishing and transportation center in Germany. Vincent had reservations at a hotel, but as we pulled up in front of the hotel we saw hookers and other sights we didn't want the boys to see. I thought it was all right for the boys to see hookers in the windows, but not on the streets. We drove around downtown Frankfurt looking for a hotel. I think we were on the wrong side of town. After driving around for 15 minutes we checked into a suite at the lovely InterContinental Hotel.

We had a room and the boys had a separate one connected to ours by a doorway. The boys dumped their Lego bags out all over the place. We ordered room service and once the waiter tiptoed over all the Legos, we ate a great meal. The last thing I heard was the clicking of Legos. I didn't know when the boys finally fell asleep; when I woke up the next morning they were still on the floor playing with Legos.

We checked out and asked the hotel clerk what activities there were for kids. The hotel clerk told us about a place where kids could eat and play.

The boys enjoy one of the free games at Vorspiel Café in Frankfurt.

We drove to the place she wrote down for us but it was the wrong address. We ate lunch at the first restaurant we saw, Vorspiel Café. *Spiel* means game and *Vor* means before. But you don't want to Google it; the images are not family-friendly.

The employees told us the address was wrong. But the restaurant had a closet full of board games, chess, and checkers. I ate potato soup and the boys ate pasta. We played a game with hopping frogs on the table. An employee told us how to play since the game's directions were in German. Playing board games was a nice change from Game Boys. We asked the waitress what she would recommend for us to do with kids.

"Go to the Senckenberg Museum, because the dinosaur bones are real," she said. We walked across the street and played "It" in a park with huge stone sculptures of plump naked women. The park looked like an outdoor museum. During our walk around the neighborhood we spotted a huge billboard of a very sexy, long red-haired, and skimpily clothed Toni Braxton. Vincent and the boys took pictures in front of the billboard. It's a guy thing.

We relax on a family-friendly statue at a park in Frankfurt.

After playing in the park, we drove to the Senckenberg Museum; it was a remarkable natural history museum with an excellent dinosaur exhibition. A family pass was only about 15 euros.

As soon as we walked into the museum we saw a huge dinosaur, but the dinosaur wasn't what caught our attention. Upstairs we turned the corner and Vincent and I were shocked. We saw an exhibit with a series of four drawings depicting human reproduction. The first drawing was a picture of a woman on her back with her legs straight up in the air and the man on top of her. We had the boys with us and this was a family museum. The drawing was clear as day. This would have been a good time to talk about sex with the boys, but the first drawing threw me off track. We entertained ourselves at the museum for a couple of hours looking at more dinosaurs and later headed off to Switzerland.

"How are you picking these cities?" I asked Vincent.

"I am just picking them (at random)."

A view of the confusing traffic patterns and signals in Central Europe.

We reached the border of Switzerland at about 10 p.m. after about a fast six-hour drive on the autobahn, Germany's super highway. Kwesi kept us entertained with stories he made up about a man named Bobby Clinton and his Lenny and Carl stories. Germany is in the European Union (EU) so we used our euros. But our euros didn't stand a chance in Switzerland. The border patrol told us it cost 30 Swiss francs to cross into Switzerland. Vincent told him we didn't have Swiss francs, only euros.

"Pull over, I'll give you change," he said in perfect English. The officer then exchanged our euros for Swiss francs, and placed a red and white sticker on the driver's side of the window.

"What city in Switzerland should we visit?" Vincent asked.

"Lucerne is beautiful," he said.

"Why can't a sister go to a part of Switzerland she heard of?" I asked Vincent.

"Zurich is just a big city just like any other big city," the border patrol officer said. So Lucerne it was. Vincent kept his laptop in the front of the car and reserved us a hotel. He got everything off the

Internet. But once we reached Lucerne we couldn't find our hotel. It was jet black outside; there may have been one street light on in the distance. We saw a shimmer of a lake where the resort was located but couldn't find the entrance.

A man just happened to be strolling down or up the street (we couldn't see) at midnight and just happened to speak English. We rolled down the window and asked him for directions to the resort. He politely told us the hotel resort was closed for the week. It was like God speaking to us with a Swiss accent. We couldn't see him and he couldn't see us. That's how dark it was outside. We wondered where was he going and why was he walking around at midnight.

Vincent had made a reservation, but the web site didn't say the hotel was closed. Two of the boys were asleep in the back of the car and Kwesi was still playing his Game Boy. Vincent got his trusty computer out again and after trying at different hotels he finally made new reservations. I suggested we call the hotel for back up. Vincent called the hotel on his cell phone and the hotel clerk was giving him instructions on what to do when we got there, just in case he went home.

"What does he mean, in case he goes home?" I asked. Sure enough, the hotel clerk had just left when we pulled up in front of the hotel. Vincent called him on his cell phone again. He told us our key was waiting for us inside the hotel. The door was locked from the outside and you had to have a code to get in. A guest in the hotel just happened to be on the computer in the lobby at 1 a.m. He buzzed us in and told us where our key was, where to park our car, and what to do. He was an American man on business. He also told me it was best to travel by train in Europe. Thanks. So there we were, in a hotel without a hotel clerk because he went home. This was a first for us. I can't imagine a hotel anywhere in the States without a front desk clerk and security

Again the boys dumped their two big bags of Legos out on the floor and played. I hoped that they would not play too loud. Vincent and I were so tired it seemed the Legos made twice as much noise

A monument to valiant Swiss soldiers.

when they hit the floor. We adults went to sleep immediately and woke up to Legos scattered everywhere.

It wasn't until morning that I discovered we were at the Hotel De La Paix, located in Lucerne, Switzerland. Lucerne is in central Switzerland.

"What is on the other side of Switzerland?" I asked Vincent, during breakfast.

"Italy."

"How far is it?"

"Two hours to the border."

"Let's go to Italy," I said.

After eating a great breakfast in the hotel we decided to take a tour of the surrounding area. We walked to the top of a steep hill to view the city and walk around the only complete city wall left in all of Europe. It was built around 1380 and used as an archive, treasury, prison, and torture chamber. We pretended to be in medieval times. We watched a man and a toddler with their legs dangling over the wall. The toddler was casually drawing in a coloring book without concern of falling over. We met an American woman who lived in Lucerne walking with her two children. We chatted and she recommended the Swiss Transport Museum.

Well, it turned out the border patrol officer was right. Lucerne is a beautiful city with gorgeous mountains and a stunning crystal-clear lake. We walked back down the hill and turned three blocks to look at a famous lion monument, "The Dying Lion of Lucerne." It was hewn out of natural rock to commemorate the massacre of hundreds of Swiss Guards in 1792, when a mob stormed the Tuileries Palace during the French revolution.

We passed a Starbucks coffee shop as we walked back to our hotel to pick up our luggage.

"How far is it to Italy?" I asked the very European-dressed male hotel clerk.

"It's two hours to the border," he said.

"Should we go to Milan?" I asked.

"You should go to Venice," he said. "Milan is just a big city. There is no place on earth like Venice. Where are you from?"

"We are from the States."

"Mountains are mountains," he said. "You can visit the Rocky Mountains in the States. You should go to Venice."

So Venice it was. One last field trip before we left Switzerland was to Verkehrshaus der Schweiz (the Swiss Museum of Transport). It is the most comprehensive traffic museum in Europe. The museum has cars, airplanes, boats, spaceships, helicopters, you name it; anything to do with transportation is here. They even had a real steam engine train that we rode on. It used real coal for fuel. The conductor would fill it up after every stop. It cost two Swiss francs; of course we were out of Swiss francs, so he let us ride free. We walked inside a real airplane. The boys took turns hang gliding. We went inside a space ship. We got on this spinning ride, but Vincent got dizzy very fast and sat in a corner while the boys toured the museum.

Nudity's much less of an issue in Europe.

We watched a movie with headphones that had about eight languages to choose from. Outside the museum were works of art. We saw a bronze statue of a naked male and female running in mid-air. We couldn't see where they were anchored. After a great day in Lucerne, with its history and beauty, we had to find an ATM machine—we needed more francs.

Ato and I ran around the corner to McDonald's, where everyone spoke English.

"McDonald's is the most famous restaurant in the world," said Kwesi.

"How do you know?" I asked him.

"Because every country we visited had a McDonald's."

I couldn't argue about that. Our McDonald's meal cost us 60 francs. We ate in the car while Vincent worked the computer again, looking for a hotel. My fear was that we would get stuck again, the way we did the night before. I drove while Vincent looked up hotels. We couldn't find Venice on the GPS anywhere. Milan was only two

A sleek helicopter at the Verkehrshaus.

hours away, but the hotel man had said "Go to Venice," that there was no place on earth like it.

Vincent said it was a four-hour drive, although the hotel man said more like six hours.

"Whenever Daddy tells us four hours, just add two more hours to the trip, so that we have time to eat and time to get lost." Kwesi said. We drove through the amazing Swiss Alps tunnels. Who dug the tunnels in the mountain? Vincent decided to tell us a story of a really bad accident inside one of the tunnels. Why then? I was mostly surprised by the houses on the side of the Alps. We couldn't see a road that lead up to the houses, but the houses were there.

It took us two days to figure out why the GPS didn't work (there are no streets in Venice, it's all water) and two days to figure out where Venice was (it's called Venezia, and we were almost there). We just drove toward Italy and hoped to see a sign or ask a border patrol officer, if there were any. Well, the border patrol in Italy just waved us on. They didn't seem to care who crossed over and who didn't. I guess the Italians figured the Swiss took care of it when

Water, water's everywhere in lovely Venice.

they saw that big red and white sticker. It became very foggy and was hard for me to see at night. Vincent was sleeping. I woke him up to tell him I couldn't see and asked if he would drive.

"You're doing all right," he said. When we end up in a canal, he'll wake up then, I thought grimly. But we arrived safe and sound.

Again, we didn't know what currency to use in Italy. Vincent thought it was euros, but since we didn't know we used credit cards to pay for the toll roads, which cost about one or two euros. I was thinking that this didn't look like the Venice seen in pictures.

"Can we go to the part with water next time?" Ato said. It wasn't until the next morning that we found out we were not in Venice, yet.

Venice is in northern Italy and made up of hundreds of islands connected by canals, walkways, and small bridges. We checked in at the nice Italian-designed NH Laguna Palace Hotel. Our floor had a lounge area with red leather chaise lounge chairs; the boys spent time relaxing. Once in our room, the boys dumped out their two bags of Legos. Need I say more?

Don't ask how I got Kwesi to stand still while I shopped.

Breakfast was included, great! It was the best ever; the buffet table had everything from eggs to chocolate cake. Vincent asked if I wanted to check out and stay at a different hotel with a pool for the boys. I said NO, we had moved around enough already. So we stayed there two nights, which was a good choice because at the end of the day we were tired.

We asked the hotel person about children's activities.

"Venice is not a city for children," she said.

Okay. She gave us directions on where and what bus to catch to get to Venice. We walked three blocks and waited for the local bus. We had to stand on the bus because it was crowded. Two Italian men were talking. I could tell that they were talking about us because they were so blatant; and I don't even understand Italian. One of the old men sneaked and rubbed his hand over Ato's hair.

The bus dropped us off and we bought tickets to catch a water bus to Venice. There are several ways to travel in Venice, a water taxi, water bus, boat, or gondola. The bus made several stops along the canal. We got off at the first stop and began our sightseeing and looked at the lovely shops and buildings with faded pastel colors.

I actually shopped for Murano cocktail glasses without the boys complaining, but I didn't push my luck. We had great pizza, the best ever, at a little pizza stand where you stood to eat. The boys had fun running up and down the steps of the old buildings and chasing pigeons.

Kofi wanted a joker's hat. We bought three joker's hats. At five euros each they were affordable souvenirs for the boys. Sure enough, there were not many children in Venice.

I saw maybe three or four kids all day. The sidewalks were busy with tourists and this was not the tourist season. The weather was a bit dreary with cloudy skies, but it didn't rain. We wore our jackets. However, we were able to capture the beauty of Venice.

Later, we ate at Burger King. We can't get away from fast food for too long. We caught a water bus back with sleepy Kofi. We got on the bus going toward the end of the canal and then it turned around. We were happily sailing along, looking at the lights on the buildings as it was beginning to turn dark. We took turns videotaping each other while the water bus sailed in the rocky waters of the Grand Canal before turning around to drop us off at the bus station. Kofi asked, "Daddy, could you videotape Venice and I watch it later because I'm sleepy?" Vincent carried Kofi the rest of the night back to the local bus. Somehow we managed to get off at the right stop and walked the three or so blocks back to the hotel.

Our unexpected trip to Venice was well worth the trip. There is no place on earth like Venice.

The world according to Vincent said it should take us nine hours to drive back to the Netherlands. Kwesi and I knew better, but we didn't say anything, we looked at each other and smiled. It would take us at least eleven hours to reach the Netherlands.

We ate our breakfast at the great buffet in the hotel, and then packed up to leave. Our GPS routed our return trip to the Netherlands. Now I know why the Italians win at skiing in the Olympics. The scene changed from houses far away on the side of the Alps to chalets with beautiful flowers overflowing in boxes outside win-

Kofi in Austria enjoying the view.

dows. Even the Alps looked different. I looked at Vincent and said, "I think we are in another country." As we crossed over into another unfamiliar territory I asked Vincent to find out where we are. Vincent asked the border patrol, "What country are we in?"

The patrol looked at us as if to say, "How come you Negroes don't know what country you are in?" He politely said, "Austria" and took our euros to pay for the toll.

The Swiss and Italian drive through their Alps. The Austrians go up and around their Alps. Vincent is an expert driver. He skillfully drove up the Alps in a spiral fashion. What goes up must come down. He skillfully drove down the other side of the Alps. He continued going up one side and back down the other side, and back up (you get the picture). If you don't get the picture there weren't guard rails. The roads are narrow, one lane going up and one lane coming down. One false move and you drop. We came to a sign that said "Pass," this means you are now between two mountains. The funny thing is the mountains in Switzerland looked different from those in Austria. In Austria, the Alps looked like giant bare and gray boul-

Tired parents after a long day.

ders on top of more boulders. The Austrian Alps were in your face. It looked as if we could reach out and touch them, unlike the distant Alps in Switzerland with grass, trees, and homes.

Again, we ate at a McDonald's, which had a gorgeous view of the Alps. There were tour buses and tourists taking pictures of the Alps. There was a gift shop with X-rated postcards. Our drive through Germany was scenic. We drove through a lot of little quaint villages and green rolling hills along the countryside.

We got stopped at the Netherlands border. Vincent asked the Dutch border patrol officer, "Why did we get stopped?" I thought it was because Vincent was driving 100 mph.

"I pulled you over because of your dark skin, you look African or Turkish and we are patrolling the border to check for passports," the officer said. "We are trying to keep the illegal North Africans out of the Netherlands."

I dug through our mess of blankets, empty potato chip bags, and candy wrappers all over the floor and found our passports. The pa-

The boys show off their McDonald's bags.

trol walked over to his computer and typed something on it and came back and told Vincent he owed some fines at the airport.

The officer said it was OK for us to go on. He said that, unlike in the States, the only way the Netherlands can check is by skin color. Little did he know it's not much different in the States. Inside the eight or so cars lined up along the roadside I noticed the people inside all had shades of brown skin, or the women had head wraps or scarves wrapped around their faces. Hmmm.

November 2005: Play Dates and Parties

In November, soon after we returned from our school break tour, the British School had a Halloween party sponsored by Outpost (Shell Oil Corp) for the expats. Halloween is not celebrated in the Netherlands.

The boys wore their costumes from Florida. Kofi was the Red Power Ranger, Ato was the Black Power Ranger, and Kwesi was Yu-Gi-Oh. I put on some face paint and went as a cat.

The party started with children telling jokes on stage; as a reward they would get a piece of candy. Ato got on stage and told a joke. I was surprised, but when it comes to candy the boys will perform. In one game, each child got to wrap another child in toilet paper so he looked like a mummy. Another game was to smell covered bowls and guest what was in the bowls. We placed our hands inside of boxes and guessed what creepy thing was inside each one.

I had to remind the Europeans that some kids (my kids) didn't know all the games. For example, they played a game called "pass

the parcel." It's a game where children sat in a circle and passed a wrapped parcel. It's wrapped many times over with wrapping paper. When the music stopped the child with the parcel unwrapped a layer of paper. The game continues until the last parcel was unwrapped; the last "unwrapper" wins the game. Another game was musical bum-bum. Like musical chairs, but without the chairs. Once the music stops you sit on your bum-bum.

* * *

Kwesi was in an after school art club, and its first meeting took place a few days later.

"You would sign me up for anything," he said.

He was right. I was grateful for the after-school programs. They provided a break from PlayStation. Ato had a play date with a classmate, so Kofi played on the computer in school while we waited for Kwesi to end his art class. He made an Egyptian mask out of clay. It looked good, particularly since art was not his strong subject.

Kofi's sixth birthday party was celebrated two months later. We held his party at Hof van Saksen, in Nooitgedacht. It was a big indoor playground with huge ball pits, little bikes to ride around on, an indoor soccer field, swimming pool, bowling alley, a restaurant, and more. I invited his whole class, all 11 children, plus six additional kids. It only cost five euros per child and included lunch with a choice of korkets, frikandels, and fries. A korket is a fried ragout of breast meat in breadcrumbs and a frikandel is a fried sausage of minced meat. The Dutch eat their French fries with mayonnaise or delicious curry ketchup and use a fork.

In our case we were allowed to pick kip nuggets (chicken nuggets) because we didn't care for the Dutch fast food choices, except chips (French fries). Now those were quite good. I ordered a Dutch birthday cake from the bakery. The baker told me to trust her because she used to live in the States and she knew how to make a similar cake, although the icing would not be the same because the Dutch icing is different.

"The Dutch birthday cakes are better," she said. "They have more filling." I told her to keep it basic because Kofi wouldn't eat it otherwise. The cake was beautifully decorated with red, white, and blue flags and candy on top. Kofi didn't like the cake but he ate the candy off the cake. Everyone else liked it.

Here's how class birthday parties worked: The Year 1 class mom collects 10 euros from each parent and purchases presents for the birthday child. That way the child can get something really big instead of a bunch of small gifts. Kofi wanted Slimecano. He had wanted this race set since last Christmas.

Vincent went back to the States for business and couldn't find Slimecano. The toy store clerk said they didn't make them anymore, it was for a promotion. If anyone sees Slimecano, get it for Kofi. He still wants it. Back to the party. Kofi did get a Hot Wheels AcceleDrome Race Set. He loved it.

He also received Legos, boxing gloves, chocolates shaped in the letter K, more chocolates, 10 euros, and more Legos. Meanwhile one of Kofi's classmates has the same birthday as his, and celebrated it on Kofi's birthday. Kofi had been pushing for a party ever since. So when he finally got one two months later, he opened all those presents at the restaurant and it was like Christmas morning. Kofi said, "When is this party over? I'm ready to go home."

Gerta's two teenage daughters came over later that day. It was the oldest girl's birthday the day before. I gave her an apple tart; I had an extra one from Kofi's party. An apple tart is the size of an extra large pizza, tastes great, and only costs seven euros. They're big, flat and round like an apple pie but without the top crust. Apple tarts are as popular as apple pie. We sat around and talked. We watched a video of my mom's 75th surprise birthday party that we had in Florida the previous year. The teenagers said they have never seen that many black people in one room at a time. There were only 20 or so family members and friends. They enjoyed watching the entertainment we had for my mom's party. They said the dancing was so passionate. The youngest girl got up and started imitating the dance moves exactly like the teenagers in the video. She was pretty good.

A few days later, the oldest Dutch teenager came over about 7:30 p.m. I was in bed looking like the wolf in granny disguise from Little Red Riding Hood. I had on my flannel gown and my scarf wrapped around my head. All three boys were in bed with me, waiting for story time, and I was tired. She came upstairs and lay across the foot of my bed. I was under the comforter and Kofi was asleep next to me. She told me about a boy she liked; how they were both shy and neither would tell the other how they felt. Typical teenage stuff. She said she had taken the tart I gave her over to the boy's house and fell down the steps with it still in the box. She said she felt so stupid. They still ate the tart.

"I am going on a field trip tomorrow," she said.

"Is the boy going on the field trip?" I asked.

"Yes."

"Take him a snack and maybe he'll get the hint that you are interested in him."

"I don't want to take him a snack," she said.

"Well, what do you want?"

"I want a kiss."

I wasn't sure what to say next. I didn't want to give her too much information or too many suggestions, being that I was not her parent. I was told, but don't know for sure, that Dutch teenagers in the Netherlands are freer to experiment with relationships, drugs, and other teenage stuff without being sneaky about it the way young people in the States have to be.

The next day, the head teacher, Mr. Underhill, at the British School called to tell me Ato wanted to stay after school to play rugby. I told him to keep all three boys. Ato signed up for everything. He was in the Christmas play; I'll tell you more about that later.

While listening to the wonderful music of Rachelle Ferrell, I successfully translated (on line) the directions for Betty Crocker brownie mix. It only took me two tries. First, I thought it was in German, but it wasn't clear so I tried French. Between both translations I was able to come up with directions.

The British School had parents come in each class and teach a cooking class to the students. You could cook or prepare anything you wanted. Sometimes there was a theme. It worked on a volunteer basis, so first I signed up for Ato's class to make cold cut combos (Subway style) and brownies. I'm not a cook. Ato's teacher wanted the parents to prepare a lunch for seventeen students.

The sun came out, and I listened to a little Kem to get me in the mood to cycle for one hour.

* * *

Kofi had a play date with Molly. We got to see another side of Assen that we hadn't seen before. I didn't realize Assen was as large as it is. I got lost picking up Kofi. We called Molly's mom and she told me how to get to her house.

When we picked up Kofi, Molly's mom said, "Molly was in one of her moods and she wouldn't play with Kofi. Kofi played with her little sister." I wanted to tell Molly's mom that Molly's not Kofi's type anyway, he likes older girls.

He had a play date with our 16-year-old neighbor, Gerta's daughter. She was six feet tall, blond, and stunning. That's the kind of play date an American boy likes.

* * *

Young scholars join Kwesi in reading Remembrance Day/St Maartens Day reports.

November 11 was St. Maartens Day (Dutch holiday) and Remembrance Day (UK holiday). It was Kwesi's Year 5/6 assembly. Assemblies were important at the school, I didn't realize. At an assembly the students present the work that they have completed up to that point. Kwesi read a paper he wrote on Neil Armstrong, the first astronaut on the moon. He read it in front of the whole school and all the parents. Every student read something.

The British students (show-offs) tried to memorize their speech and speak "proper" English but struggled. The American kids read their reports from their papers and also struggled. It was like watching Tony Blair, then-prime minister of the UK and former President George Bush, speaking at the same event. I'm joking, it wasn't that bad. Remembrance Day was also talked about at the assembly. It is something like our Veteran's Day.

Several students talked about Anne Frank. Some students wrote reports on Dr. Martin Luther King, Jr.

It was a busy day, because we also had the Year 3 cooking class. Tami, another parent, and I baked brownies and prepared hoagies with the class in the kitchen. The class was divided into two groups. We were in charge of the cooking class, without a teacher present. It went quite well. I supervised the brownies with half the students. Tami supervised the other half of the students making hoagies. Plus

St. Maarten's Day group ready to collect treats—looks a lot like Halloween.

we gave them a Dutch version of Kool-Aid and a bag of chips. Cooking class was a real nice addition to the curriculum.

At the end of the assembly, all the students went to their classroom and brought back their lanterns that they made in class. Then they lit the lanterns by putting a flashlight inside. Kofi's version of the story of St. Maarten was about a rich man who gave half his coat to a poor man. The Dutch said he did more, but that's the basis of the story. St. Maarten's Day is only celebrated in the north. Traditionally, children walk from house to house and sing a Dutch song. In return they receive a sweet treat. It's something like Halloween but without the costumes and horror. Instead of "trick or treat" it's called "walking for St. Maarten." It was funny watching the American kids sing a song in Dutch to receive candy. The person opens the door and waits for the kids to sing the whole song in Dutch and then and only then does he or she give the kids candy.

Can you imagine how long this took for every person in every house to wait until the song was finished? I drove the boys and their

Singing for their supper—the boys get treats while walking for St. Maarten.

American friend, Donnie Jones, to the other side of Assen to meet at Gabriel's house, where a group of parents from school gathered, and we all went together. We were a big crowd, so we broke up into an older and a younger group.

The parents that I walked with wanted to keep all my boys together. Kwesi and Donnie started complaining (as if I cared) that they wanted to go with the older kids. Then Ato started complaining that he wanted to go with the younger kids. Kwesi and Donnie, along with a parent, went with the older kids. I stayed with Ato and Kofi's younger group.

We got home late and most kids had already collected their sweets. I told Donnie and Kwesi not to behave that way again—after all, I didn't have to take them in the first place. We stopped at the home of Martha, a neighborhood friend, just so she could see the boys and hear them sing in Dutch. And yeah, she laughed and waited until the whole song was over before she gave each smiling boy a nice-sized bag of candy. They were happy. We only gave out a few sweets because we were out collecting candy.

* * *

Ato was dropped off at a play date with Josh. Play dates are huge and I can't stress that enough. The boys have been to more play dates in the Netherlands than in their whole lifetimes combined. We picked Ato up at 11:30 a.m. because Josh was going to the Sinterklaas parade in downtown Assen.

Vincent decided against us going because he felt it was racist in nature. That's how I saw it, too. Sinterklaas is an old tradition dating back to medieval times. Sinterklaas is an old white man, like Santa Claus. To me, he looked more like the pope instead of Santa Claus; he wore a red robe with a gold and white mitre. That observation didn't go over well in the Protestant Netherlands. His helper (servant) is called Zwarte Piet, which translates in English to Black Pete. The Dutch put on blackface, jet-black opaque stockings, and afro wigs. The blackface is exaggerated. Zwarte Piet plays music and gives candy out to children. The tradition goes that Zwarte Piet is black because he came from Spain on a ship with Sinterklaas and the Moors dominated Spain at that time.

The second reason they say Zwarte Piet is black is because he went down the chimney so many times that the black soot covered him. The Dutch tell their children if they misbehave Zwarte Piet will take them back to Spain and they won't get toys. I've seen babies and toddlers with their little faces covered with black makeup and wearing the whole Zwarte Piet costumes and gear.

I can only think of Spike Lee's movie "Bamboozled." Maybe if the Dutch saw it they would understand better.

The Dutch claim that they're not racist the way some people are in the States. But folks from Suriname, South Africa, or North Africa would disagree. My white American friend living in the Netherlands said if she was black she wouldn't let her kids see the parade. She was surprised that another girlfriend of ours from Nigeria was taking her children to the parade.

A swarm of Zwarte Piets. The Dutch loved them; we didn't get it.

I have noticed that some small Dutch children stared at us when we were out and about. I think it's because they haven't seen many black people, especially in the northern part of the country. I hoped that they didn't think I was Zwarte Piet. My Dutch neighbor said that Dutch children will ask their parent if that is Zwarte Piet when they see a man with dark skin. For the record, Dutch people of the world, blackface and the whole Zwarte Piet thing is offensive.

We spent the afternoon eating at McDonald's looking at the various Zwarte Piets coming in and out of the restaurant. Later the boys went on a play date with the teenage girls next door and played PlayStation. Some things are universal.

Sunday, we ate a late lunch at Van der Valk Hotel in Assen. It has a play area for children. All stores, businesses, etc., have play areas for children. It worked out well; the boys played while the food was being prepared. Vincent gave them walkie-talkies so we could stay in touch. The hotel had one of the few restaurants that the boys preferred over McDonald's. Dessert was ice cream in a plastic cup in the shape of an animal that the kids got to keep. We eventually collected every animal, some twice. Later, we went bike riding in the woods

The boys rode ahead looking for a hill (good luck). The Netherlands are as flat as Florida. There was a low-grade hill under the train tracks. By the time Vincent and I reached the boys, Kofi had crashed into a brick wall. He didn't get hurt, but his American bike broke into two pieces. Vincent carried the bike parts back home as he pedaled his bike. Kofi rode on the back of Kwesi's bike. We went home early; it got dark that far north at about 5 p.m. Vincent was the only one with working bike lights. The rest of us didn't have lights, but the Dutch take bike lights very seriously. You can get fined for not having bike lights and that would have been four fines.

* * *

The following day was rugby practice (non-contact). The Kwapong boys can't take a hit. The boys enjoyed rugby. Ato was the only kid who wore a coat and gloves during practice.

I went walking with my new best American friend, Tami, Ato's classmate's mom, in the cold and wet weather. It was not as bad as I thought it would be. It rained a lot, so it was best to stay on my exercise routine and not let the weather determine if I went walking.

Tami had been in the Netherlands a year or so and she was helpful with a lot of information about school, the country, who's who and traveling around Europe. She was the first person to introduce herself to me at school. She invited all three boys to her son's birthday party within days of meeting her. Vincent, the boys and I rode our bikes to decide if her house was in bike riding distance or if we should drive. We were looking at their house for an address, like spies, to see if we had the right house and she came out and invited us inside. We instantly became friends. Tami had many play dates for her sons. She is originally from Minnesota. Her husband is from the Ukraine.

Every morning Tami needed a cup of strong coffee before we went walking. Sometimes I would have coffee with her. I needed to keep coffee in check. I didn't want to develop any habits, good, bad, or otherwise. Kwesi had a play date at home with Robert and Donnie. Donnie stayed with us every day after school for a week. His dad picked him up when he got off work. His father worked at the same company as Vincent. His mom was in the States and was expected back later that week. Both boys were good to have around. Robert's mom is from Zimbabwe and his dad is from the Netherlands.

Robert speaks English and Dutch. He was in Year 6, along with Kwesi. Ato and Kofi had a play date at home set for next week. This play date thing is weekly.

I watched my favorite TV show, "Desperate Housewives." The funny thing is that when I was in Florida, I didn't watch it at all. But when your choices of English shows are limited, you adapt really fast. When we first arrived in the Netherlands, we watched Will Smith's, "Fresh Prince of Bel Air," until it stopped being broadcast in the Netherlands.

Another cold, wet, and sunless day. To say cloudy was an understatement—days without sun were common that time of year. The sky was a blanket of gray or a dull blue. I went walking despite the weather.

I didn't get a lot of peace Wednesday because it was a half day, the boys got out of school at noon. It's a European thing. Cherri, the school expert, said it's a good thing. She says the States need half days because the teachers need the extra time for professional development.. As luck would have it, when we first returned to the States, we wound up in a school district in Florida with half-day Wednesdays.

I didn't walk because Tami canceled. So instead, I did an abs routine to a music video channel here called The Box. I watched an interesting and powerful video by Janet Jackson. I didn't recognize her in the video (although it looked like Janet) because of the nature of the video. It was filmed in an African night club, or the setting was an African night club. Why was that important? Well, when you are in another country anything familiar is celebrated.

I cycled to town with my Suriname neighbor, Martha. She was extremely helpful in showing me the best places to shop. I was on a budget to spend 150 euro per week. If money was left over it was saved for holidays and vacation travels. So far so good.

* * *

A week later, Vincent and I went to the boys' parent-teacher meetings. We started with Kofi. I wanted to get Kofi in Year 2. I asked his teacher "Why is Kofi in the Pull-Ups class?

"What is the Pull-Ups class?" she asked.

"Everyone in Kofi's class looks like they are wearing Pull-Ups," I said. Pull-Ups are the intermediate undergarments children wear as they move from diapers to drawers and learn to control their bathroom needs. The school said it was not their fault that Kofi was tall. He entered Year 1 as a beginner reader, so they kept him in Year 1.

Kofi was in speech class for a short time in Florida. He talked like Ato when he was talking to Ato and pronounced his words clearer when he talked with everyone else. The school tested Kofi for speech and recommended that he take speech therapy, due to the fact that he didn't pronounce "th" correctly and he didn't pronounce the last letters in his words. But I couldn't get our USA health insurance to pay for it.

Kofi was doing very well. He was in the top reading group and the top math group. I'm not surprised. He had done most of the work in South Florida at his private kindergarten. He was reading surprisingly well. His teacher said that he was sad and lonely at the beginning of the school year, but since then he had made friends and was excited about going to school.

Ato's meeting was a surprise. He was in the gifted program in the States, but Ato's teacher said he was average. His teacher also said Ato was lonely at the beginning of the school year. He would follow Kwesi around the school playground at recess. Now Ato had his own friends and got along really well.

Kwesi's class work was average. Again, that was a surprise because in the States he was at the top of his class. I was successful in getting Kwesi into the Year 6 class. He also was lonely at the beginning of the school year. I asked all three teachers why they didn't tell us. They all felt there was no need for concern. After leaving the meetings, I decided to return to a more structured routine, similar to what we had in Florida. I made them read more with a timer to keep them focused. I demanded higher standards from the boys, which was hard to do because the British School didn't give out much homework.

The boys usually completed their school work in class, which I couldn't monitor. I didn't see the results until after the work was completed and graded.

The Europeans felt that after school was family time. But I kept stressing that Kwesi practice writing cursive and using the dictionary for spelling. Kofi wrote some numbers and letters backwards, so we worked on those. Ato was concentrating on writing longer papers. I tracked their progress.

I'm not sure why Ato's tests scores were average. I thought about the British language barrier. For example, the word rubber in Britain means eraser; in the States it means something else, you know? The fact that he was new to the British system may have played a factor. If Ato pronounced a word wrong it was marked against him even though I told the school he was in speech class in the States. Their difficulties could have been due to our difficult beginning here, before we solved our transportation problems.

* * *

Next up was Year 3 Assembly. The theme was science. Each child had to speak in front of the class, which builds their character. Children in the British School were trained to enjoy public speaking. Ato had a play date with Josh after school. I went walking after the assembly on a very sunny but cold day. The only housework for that day was ironing. Yahoo!

That Saturday, we woke up to frost everywhere. I started the boys on house assignments; it went well. They didn't know yet that their chores were every day. Kwesi complained but who cared. We spent the afternoon in the children's section at the Drents Museum. The boys enjoyed themselves. The Netherlands is truly a child-friendly society. The museum staff informed me that I could leave the boys in the children's museum while I visited the rest of the facility and come back for them later. Once I found that out, Vincent and I went off on our own. The boys got "passports" and went around the museum collecting information with help from the staff, because the boys couldn't read Dutch, and filled out the booklets. At the end of the session when their passport booklets were complete the boys received candy.

We learned some interesting facts about the Netherlands during our visit. Fact one was the Dutch call their grandfathers Opa 1, Opa 2, and so on and so on all the way to Opa 3000. Their history dates that far back. We use grandfather, great grandfather, etc. The boys cut leather with a rock, the way it was done 1,000 years ago. I got them a treat for behaving well. We ate lunch in the museum restaurant and we ordered several 7-Up drinks, tasty tosti (ham and cheese on toast) and the best ever chips (French fries). The restaurant gave all children free ice cream.

Sunday was another gray and dull day. We stayed in the whole day and the boys played Legos, computer games and completed their home assignments. I washed three loads of clothes and still had more. The washing machines in Europe were kind to clothes; the regular wash cycle was gentle and longer than in the States, where the machines are faster and harder on your clothes. In Europe it seemed I had all day to wash and iron clothes. In the States I was always rushing around to do something else and washing and ironing was squeezed in.

The bad weather stayed with us through the month, which is probably why weather is one cause of depression in the Netherlands.

I showed up at Tami's home and she said she was not walking, but invited me in for coffee. Can't turn down coffee, can I? We talked and just enjoyed each other's company. It is funny who your friends become when in a different country. But I would choose Tami as a friend anywhere in the world. Sadly, she moved to Russia at the end of the school year after her husband got a promotion.

* * *

On my birthday, I chose not to have a cake. Happy birthday to me. The boys eat cake sometimes and sometimes they don't. I didn't want to get stuck eating a whole cake again.

Kofi had a play date with Mustafa. Since I didn't know my way around Assen, I followed his mom home to see where they lived (so I could pick up Kofi that afternoon).

I was invited to stay for breakfast. That was very cool. We really can learn to live and love others who are different from us. I accepted my invitation into a culture and world that I knew primarily from CNN. She was Muslim, from Iraq. She had been an engineer in Iraq. She first told me her English was not good and if she said something offensive, please accept her apologies. Her English was better than my Arabic.

We had tea. She offered me breakfast, but I saw a cake and asked for a slice of cake. She gave me a funny look, so I said I'll have the toast and cheese she offered. She gave me toast, cheese, and cake. She told me that different head coverings may be either cultural or religious. She removed her head wrap. It was the first time I saw her uncovered. Her dark hair fell past her shoulders. She said her hair was for her husband to see only. I learned that she felt that the U.S. should stay in Iraq and that Saddam Hussein needed to be removed. (This was before he was captured and executed.) If the U.S. pulled out now, she said, the Iraqis would kill each other. There were too many different groups and they all hated each other. As I was leaving she said that she hadn't expected me to eat so much because of my size. OK, now that may be a bit offensive, but I let it go.

Vincent brought me roses. We didn't have a vase. We went to a few stores, but they were closed. We ended up at Praxis, a store like Home Depot or Lowe's. We found a nice vase. It was the only store open. The stores in Assen closed at 5 or 6 p.m. instead of 9 or 10 p.m., the way they do in the States. I had to plan well to accommodate for the early store closing. Speaking of planning, I decided to practice baking sugar cookies. Year 5/6 cooking day was coming up.

We were invited to Cynthia and Bob Howards' house (he was one of the managers at Vincent's job) for Thanksgiving dinner in Groningen. We arrived cold, wet, and late due to traffic and rain. However, everything worked out very nicely. The dinner was a traditional Thanksgiving feast with turkey, stuffing, and pumpkin pies. We entertained the Howards as best we could without looking like idiots in the eyes of the manager. The boys were well behaved. What more could you ask for? The other American family that was invited didn't show, which meant that more drama was to follow. You never decline a dinner invitation to the manager's house. It felt like a scene from "Desperate Housewives."

December 2005: Holiday Season

Ato had a play date at home with Ivan, Felipe, and John. I had six boys in a European car. I put four in the back. Kwesi and Ato sat in the front seat. Ato was only supposed to invite two playmates, but a little boy ran up to me after school and asked if he could come over. I said yes, thinking that it was Felipe but it was John. I still get the European children mixed up. They played with Legos and computer games and had big fun. Next week was Kofi's play date. He had already invited too many classmates.

On Saturday, we woke up to our first snowy day in the Netherlands. The boys went outside in the back yard at 7:55, before daylight. They were too excited to wait for sunrise. They built a snowman with a carrot-stick nose. The snow was pretty from my seat by the window.

Vincent went to the bank by bike. Why he waited until it snowed to ride a bike, I'll never know. He claimed the bike routes were plowed. He received bad information. I listened to Kem, an R&B artist, and tried to remember last week's events that needed recording because I didn't journal every day. The boys came inside for a short time. Children can handle just about anything. They put on their wet coats and went out to continue playing in the snow.

We were struggling with what to do for Christmas. Where should we go? Who should we visit? The choices were endless. I'm always in favor of family. A change of music was in order. John Legend's "When It's Cold Outside" fit the bill that day.

* * *

Kofi went to a Sinterklaas concert with Years 1 and 2 classes. He enjoyed himself. It was also Kofi's long-awaited play date at home. We had five more children than planned. One of Kofi's schoolmates had to go to swimming class, so Kofi ran around the whole school yard asking parents if their child could come over for a play date to replace the kid that couldn't come over. He asked a woman I had never met, who said yes. She followed me to the house so she could pick up her two boys later. This somewhat surprised me because we were strangers, but I guess she figured the boys knew each other and the school had our records.

Meantime, Ato ran over to another mom with two boys also and asked her and she also said yes. We had a total of seven boys, including my three, and one small girl from the Philippines. The girl ruled; she played "boys'" computer games like no tomorrow. Thank goodness, they were a good bunch of kids.

The next day Archie came over to play with Kwesi. Archie was the boy whose party we had missed last week because the invitation stayed in Kwesi's backpack. To make up for missing the party, I scheduled a play date. The noise level of European boys was incredibly low compared to boys' noise in the States. That's when I realized how loud Kofi and Ato played. I hoped they didn't give the boy a headache. He was mild-mannered with a British accent. Archie said he used to fight like Ato and Kofi with his sister when he was little. He was only about eleven years old. On Thursday Kofi woke up and didn't get a Sinterklaas gift.

I told him it was because he hadn't put the carrot and a bowl of water out for the flying horse. Plus he was supposed to sing a song.

So Kofi was on it that night. He sang his heart out and put his carrot and bowl of water right in front of the fireplace. So I had to do some wrapping. The boys carried their shoes to the Albert Heinz grocery store and left them so that Sinterklaas would leave a gift inside each shoe.

Sinterklaas was so much fun once you got past Zwarte Piet. I had four gifts to buy that day. Ato was going to a birthday party for two kids. I had to buy Kwesi's Sinterklaas gift for the grab bag, plus the boy's birthday party that we missed. You guessed it. We bought more Legos for presents.

* * *

That afternoon I was out and about with Martha. Later she said her husband couldn't believe how long we stayed out since we only went to one or two stores. I had a field trip briefing at the school that afternoon. Kwesi's class, Years 5/6 were going on a field trip to the water treatment plant.

The teacher told the volunteer parents what to expect and that each parent would have two kids to chaperone. Martha gave the boys a bag of Sinterklaas papernotens, tiny cinnamon cookies. During Christmas, candy is added to the bags of cookies. Martha told the boys that they were from Sinterklaas. The boys didn't like the candy, but they loved the papernotens. This satisfied Kofi's wish for a gift from Sinterklaas. Kofi still wanted a Hot Wheels Slimecano.

Martha said the Dutch kids got gifts up to December 5th. I think it was five days of gifts starting on December 1st. On December 5th the children got something big. However, the boys received a small Lego set on December 5th. We still had Christmas to consider. So every day I thought of small gifts for Sinterklaas to put in the boys' shoes. Kofi still believed in the magic of Christmas, Sinterklaas, Kwanzaa, Hanukah and any other holiday that would get him gifts. Kwesi and Ato knew the deal.

On Dec. 2 the boys got their first Sinterklaas gifts. Kofi made everyone paper shoes. He learned how to make them in school and carefully placed them by the fireplace. He said it was a Dutch tradition. The boys received little cars with a booster in their paper shoes. Kofi took his car to school for show and tell.

* * *

Year 1 Assembly was too cute. This was Kofi's class and they presented their work to their parents. They made a toy shop in class after visiting a toy museum. They also made a moving puppet "Jumping Jack." They sang a song. The headmaster said he read that the Lego Company was having problems with sales and that he was worried about the lack of future engineers and architects.

"Children won't have the basic foundation of building," he said. Not with the Kwapong boys around! They had a zillion Legos and were looking to get more every chance possible. We supported Lego as if we had a direct link to their bottom-line financial sheet. I usually buy Legos for birthday gifts.

Ato went over to John's for a play date. Kofi went over to Joey's for a play date. Kwesi and I had some time alone, which was needed. Guess what? We played with Legos.

Sure enough, Zwarte Piet was at the grocery store passing out treats when we went to pick up the boys' shoes. Then, the next day, he was at school with Sinterklaas. They both had on velvet. Sinterklaas had a long red velvet cloak and a gold cane. Zwarte Piet had on red velvet knickers with puffy sleeves. I guess the outfits vary.

A few days later we went to a Connect International Christmas party held at Huys van Bunne Drents, complete with old school Santa Claus, lights, decorations, and an elf with presents for all the children. The children sat around old St. Nick. He called each child by name one at a time. They sat on his lap while the elf gave each child a gift.

We had a great dinner buffet that included everything from turkey, ham, roast beef, salads, vegetables, cheeses, and breads to an ice cream buffet.

I hear it's your birthday!—Kwesi turns 10.

A white-bearded fat man in a red suit represented the USA and a white-bearded tall man in a red robe represented the Netherlands. Not much difference.

A week later, each class presented a play. Kofi's class danced and he got down real low doing the twist. Their theme was the beach. Kofi wore his swim trunks, goggles and had sun screen on his nose. Ato's class wore winter coats and I can't remember the theme. Kwesi's class was dressed up and I can't remember that

75

theme either. He had on a white button-down shirt. Another class had angels, more of a Christmas theme.

That weekend, Kwesi turned 10. We held a party at home. All his classmates were invited, along with family friends. With the help of my teenage neighbor, we blew up balloons and tacked them in the doorway to the dining room. Each child decorated a small Christmas tree to take home. We played video games and Legos and danced. The teenager brought over a music CD. We made ice cream sundaes. The boys played soccer in the yard. One child had to leave to take horseback riding lessons. She left and came back to the party.

January 2006: Sea Cruise!

On Christmas Day, we revealed our plan to the boys. We would go on a cruise. Kofi yelled and screamed when he found out that we were planning an 18-day cruise. "Does an 18-day cruise take 18 days?" he asked.

"Why don't we drive to the airport and catch a plane to Florida?" he said. "Eighteen days will take forever."

I had my own set of questions. No point in asking about them then. It was our first cruise and we bravely went on an 18-day cruise, without prior knowledge of cruising, with three boys ages ten, seven, and six. I wasn't sure if the boys would be able to handle it, but we couldn't change the plans.

"Pack light," Vincent said. That was impossible. Vincent and I tried to be smart this time. We drove to Amsterdam and stayed overnight at the Hilton airport hotel, then caught an early flight to Genoa, Italy. We didn't want to take a chance and miss the cruise

The boys didn't appreciate Genoa's beauty, but they weren't taking the pictures!

ship. Vincent had a habit of arriving late at airports and missing flights.

The flight was smooth. Some people were dressed for business. It was a short flight, about one hour, and then we landed in Italy. We didn't know Italian and getting around was interesting, especially on Christmas Day. The good news was someone always spoke English, no matter where we ended up.

We stayed overnight in Genoa, which was absolutely beautiful. It's a coastal town and we watched the ships cruise in and out of port. Genoa has beautiful places of worship, monuments, fountains, and many historical sites. Genoa is believed to be the birthplace of Christopher Columbus. Who knew? We walked the empty cobble-stone streets. We took plenty of pictures, while the few Italians on the street looked on. The ancient architecture was splendid. The boys wanted to know why everything looked old and run down. I told them they were called ruins. They didn't see the beauty in the ancient architecture, but it's there. Kofi pronounced Italy as It-la-ty our entire trip.

Our hotel was nice. We picked a chain hotel since it was our first time in Italy. Sometimes it's best to stick with what you know until you become familiar with European travel. Our hotel rooms were not together, so we split up. Vincent had two boys. I took the other boy. The boys wanted to sleep in their own room by themselves down the hall, but I knew they wouldn't last 10 minutes alone.

I noticed the Italian style immediately. Some Italians were wearing fur coats. I hadn't seen fur coats in the Netherlands. Men and women were dressed so stylishly. Even the older Italian women had on sharp fur coats. We caught a local bus from the hotel and walked down a hill to the tourist booth for information. We decided to visit an aquarium. Acquario Di Genova was located on the coast and is the largest aquarium in Italy and the second biggest aquarium in Europe.

The layout was great. Various water creatures were swimming over our heads in glass aquariums. We ate at McDonald's.

The next day we patiently waited in line to board the beautiful MSC (Mediterranean Shipping Company) Opera. The MSC Opera is 830 feet long, 96 feet wide, and has ten decks for guests. All went well. We walked onto the ship, it looked like the Titanic

A family portrait at sea.

Everything was shining and spectacular! The waiters were dressed spotlessly in all white. The majority of the staff looked the same, Asian. An Asian crew on an Italian cruise ship? Go figure. One waiter said the shipping company liked Asians because they always looked like they were smiling. MSC *Opera*'s crew of 700 came from about 30 countries, principally Italy. I got this off the daily program. The crew just didn't look Italian, but maybe it was like the USA, where there isn't an "American" look.

The boys were already running up and down the steps. They ran to the top of the stairs and jumped off. We quickly stopped that game. Being put off a ship in Europe was not our idea of fun.

We had two cabins next to each other. One boy stayed with Vincent and two stayed with me or vice versa. It wasn't a honeymoon, it was a "familymoon." This was the best we could do with small boys and late planning. We loved our cabin even though we did not have an ocean view.

Every morning we received a daily program, tour magazine and port information. In the programs were the events for the day, excursion information, dinner times, what to wear at dinner times, activities, parties, and other important information. Our first morning, we had a lifeboat exercise. We went to our muster station and met the crew on the dock. They went over the life-saving exercises about what to do in an emergency. Put your life vest on and step into the ocean. Do not jump! You don't want to wake up the sharks.

Our first stop was Valencia. We had just enough time for one field trip.

We only had one day to explore Valencia. It's Spain's third largest city, famous for its oranges and as the place where Rodrigo Diaz de Vivar, called El Cid and El Campeador, defeated the Moors in 1094 on behalf of the Christians. The city fell to the Almoravids in 1102. Following the Moorish domination, in 1238 James I of Aragon finally conquered the city and founded the Kingdom of Valencia.

.

Valencia's City of Arts and Sciences

Our choices were between the Oceanographic Museum or The City of Arts and Sciences. Since we visited the Aquarium in Genoa, we decided on the science museum. The weather was clear and cool. We walked about eight blocks to the museum. A woman traveling alone from the cruise ship walked with us, she was also visiting the museum. The science district was amazing! In front of us were museum buildings of various unique shapes and sizes made out of laminated glass. Each museum was as unique and futuristic as the next; one had a rectangle shape made out of wire and glass, one had a huge glass dome and another had mirror spheres all over it. We couldn't decide what to do, but settled on the science museum because it was hands on and the boys would love it.

Everything was in Spanish, of course. We had a bit of a struggle trying to buy tickets because we couldn't speak the language. Someone went and got the one employee that spoke English. He helped us buy our tickets and told us about the museum. We toured all three glass floors of exhibits and did everything there was to do that involved future technology, modern science, and fun. The boys even

Funchal is the capital city of Madeira, a beautiful island in the Atlantic Ocean.
It's closer to Africa than it is to Europe, but it's culturally and politically European. Madeira was colonized in the year 1420 by Prince Henry the Navigator.
Under the Portuguese constitution Madeira was granted the right to self-determination.

went rock climbing. Our favorite exhibits were kicking a soccer ball that measured speed and the track and field exhibit with a large picture of Jackie Joyner Kersee racing. Our speed was timed against hers in the exhibit.

By New Year's Eve we were in Portugal. Our challenge was for all five of us to stay up until midnight to enjoy "one of the most beautiful fireworks displays of the world."

According to the Guinness Book of Records, it was also the largest fireworks display in the world. We were never able to stay awake on New Year's Eve. We took a nap after dinner so that we could wake up in time to watch the fantastic display of fireworks from the ship. It was cold, so we wore our coats. We ate at the New Year's Eve Grand Buffet. It *was* grand and so were the fireworks, which lit up the entire side of the island. Other cruise ships' passengers were watching the fireworks also.

The ship's daily program reminded us to set our watches back one hour. Time is important if you don't want the ship to leave without you. Funchal sits on the bay with mountains in the background. The next day we walked up a long steep hill to sightsee and shop. It wasn't a far walk from the ship, but a strenuous walk. The boys bought baseball caps with the word Madeira on the front for their souvenirs. Flowers were everywhere and the weather was warm.

Vincent and I spent the next morning exercising while the boys went to the Buffalo Bill's Children Center. They played video games and other kid activities and could have stayed all day.

Miniature golf—later I wanted to use my club on a certain shipmate.

From the coast of Portugal we sailed across the Atlantic, seeing nothing but water for five days straight. It was weird. We landed in Grenada on January 7, and from the ship we could see the lush, green mountains of the island. The boys wanted to go hiking.

We played mini-golf in the hot sun on the top deck, while we waited to be called off the ship. Playing mini-golf with five people took a long time.

While I was in the lobby returning our golf clubs, Ato was jumping around (as little kids do) in the lobby. An old European man walked right into him with his cane. The old man pushed Ato. I saw stars. It took a lot not to beat him. I told Vincent and he said, "You should have said something to the man." Again, a sister to the rescue. Once off the ship I politely told the old man not to push my kid again. First, he acted like he couldn't speak English. I told his companions and they translated.

"The boy ran into me," he said.

"You ran into the boy," I snapped.

He apologized. That was just one example of some of the arrogance of some Europeans. And they call us the Ugly Americans.

Some Europeans would walk into us, as if we should move out of their way, like in the States. You could forget waiting in line. I think the Europeans don't understand queuing. Maybe in different countries, but on the Italian cruise ship, they would just walk up to the counter and step in front of us while we would wait for our turn. Manners weren't their strong characteristic on the ship. That didn't ruin my day. It just made me more aware.

Granada was inhabited by the Carib Indians, before Columbus "discovered" the island in 1498. England and France fought to control the island. Meanwhile, England transported enslaved Africans. In 1795, Julian Fedon, a black planter, lead a violent slave rebellion, taking control of Granada, but was crushed by the British. Tension remained high until slavery was abolished in 1834. Granada gained independence from England in 1974.

When we told a local that we wanted to go hiking, he said, "The bugs would eat you this time of year." We went to Grand Anse Beach instead of hiking. Granada was still recovering from Hurricane Emily. Many buildings still needed repairs.

We stopped at South City Plaza near the beach, where the boys bought themselves toys and Chinese checkers. After shopping for their toys they weren't that interested in the beach. We ate lunch at a restaurant on the beach—you'd think with all that food on the ship, we wouldn't be hungry. It was a beautiful beach with typical white sand and blue water.

Ato read every morning the port information that explained a brief history about each island. Kwesi wanted to know why everyone looked Jamaican. I told him they looked like us.

"Africans were transported against their will and placed on these islands as slaves and taken to different parts of the world," I said. Not a pleasant story but one that must be told.

Life is a beach in the Caribbean

One of the most beautiful islands we visited was Isla de Margarita, which is part of Venezuela. The Guaiqueries Indians called the island Para-guachoa, meaning abundance of fish. However, the Spanish "dis-coverers" called it La Mararita be-cause of the abundance of pearls found. As usual, they were just looking for the loot.

After a pleasant day on the beach, we headed back to the ship. The taxi driver gave us a short tour of St. George. There were tiny shops along the way. The port of Granada had really nice shops. We finally bought a few gifts. The beautiful sale clerk was amazed that the boys looked so much alike. She thought they were triplets.

She talked Vincent into buying a bottle of alcohol with some herbs and spices in it. It was supposed to be good for his manhood, you know what I mean? I guess you could say it's Viagra in a bottle. "We'll see about that," I said.

Granada is known for its spices. I settled for a nice jar of nutmeg jelly with the spices in it. I had a ton of gifts to buy, as I counted them on a sheet of paper, it seemed impossible to cover them all at this point.

I started buying bottles of wine but the bags were getting heavy already. I had Dutch neighbors, friends, and relatives in Pittsburgh that helped out with the boys, and friends in Florida. I couldn't keep up so I stopped buying gifts before I got started.

Our next stop was Margarita, an island off the north shore of Venezuela. The center of town was quite far from the dock. We took a local bus ride to town, with the encouragement of a couple traveling on the ship; the wife was from Panama and she spoke Spanish. Otherwise, we would have still been sitting on a rock in Margarita wondering what to do. The bus ride included about twelve other tourists. Our plan was to go horseback riding with the boys.

The boys' favorite shop during the trip.

We drove through dry land with just patches of grass and other sparse vegetation that could survive in the heat. In the far distance were hills covered with lush green vegetation. We were told to meet back at the bus in about two hours. Kwesi reported in the video camera what we saw and where we were. We took pictures and window shopped.

About 10 minutes into our self-made sightseeing trip, Kofi spotted a Power Rangers shirt in the window of a shop, and the rest was history. Ato and Kwesi also wanted a Power Ranger shirt. Even though

Columbus landed on Martinique in 1502 and named the island in honor of St. Martin. The Carib Indians living on the island before Columbus called it Matinino or Madinina. The island was claimed by France in 1635 and officially annexed by the King of France in 1674. On May 22, 1848, slavery was abolished.

Kwesi was a bit too old for Power Rangers, we bought him one anyway. Kofi called his outfit a Power Ranger suit because they bought

Discussing our options.

the matching denim pants with a Power Ranger patch on one knee. We found a really interesting shop close to the end of our stay there. I could have stayed in this store the whole two hours. Unfortunately, I cannot remember the name of the town. We ran back to the bus within a minute of leaving time.

I bought a few gifts at the port. There were a lot of really interesting vendors there. The boys bought watches from the vendors at the port. At dinner the waiters laughed when the boys showed them their new watches. The waiters enjoyed seeing and talking to the boys every night. They would ask them questions ranging from Game Boys to Vincent's high tech gadgets. It was probably a nice change of people for them. I bet that we were the first black family with three boys on the *Opera*.

Next, we stopped at Martinique. The official language was French, although English was spoken in the tourist areas. Many islanders often speak Creole. The currency is euros but dollars were accepted.

Vincent stopped at the tourist booth and asked for information.

La Martinique Reconnaissante

Not knowing what to do, we walked 20 minutes into town looking for a bank. We always ran out of euros.

We ran into one of the other African-American couples. There were a total of three black couples including Vincent and me and our three black boys on the entire ship. They said they were just looking around and going to visit a museum. So we decided to do the same. The museum opened at 1p.m.. We were early. We took pictures together. At noon we ate at KFC for lunch. The boys ran upstairs looking for a play center. I found out that I left my wallet in our cabin.

Vincent left KFC to get euros out of the money machine. The Musee Departmental d'Archeologie et de Prehistoire was filled with pre-Columbus artifacts. Every island has a version of Columbus and how his voyages affected the people living there before and after. I don't think the boys enjoyed this field trip, but it was educational.

Later that day, Vincent told us about a volcano we could have seen. I called him "Mr. Day Late and a Dollar Short." He's a walking encyclopedia, he has great information, but by the time he shared what he knew it was too late. He knew how much the boys like to climb and explore. The boys like anything that can blow up or was blown up. They are true Americans. Vincent said the person in the tour information booth told him we didn't have enough time to go to the volcano. This is what I get for not doing research about the places we visited beforehand.

Before boarding the ship, we looked around at the shops near the port. I told the boys to pick out postcards. They soon huddled in a corner giggling. When I looked at them they stopped. When I turned my back they giggled again. I walked over to see what they were giggling about. Ato wanted to buy a post card with a picture of a model with a thong on and her back to the camera exposing her rear end. To his surprise, I let him buy it.

Our next port of call was St. Maarten/St. Martin. The island is divided into two parts. We docked in the port of Philipsburg, capital of the Dutch part of the island. We entered a table soccer tournament on the ship.

Our Italian Stallion, the M.S.C. Opera.

A European couple switched partners so that Kwesi played with the husband and his wife played with Ato. I lost real fast. Kwesi's team came in second. We are a competitive family; we wanted to win.

My goal was to stop the boys from whining every time they lost. Oh yeah, the object of the game was to have fun. The good news was that the boys were writing in their own journals.

Ato was more prone to illness than the other two boys. But Kofi was not to be outdone. Kofi showed me his old sore. He did have an old cut. I gave him Tylenol anyway. I usually pack a small suitcase full of medicine.

A treaty dividing St. Maarten/St. Martin was signed in 1648. The northern side is French (St. Martin) and the southern side is Dutch (St. Maarten). The languages are Dutch, Papiamento, and English on the Dutch side and French and English on the French side.

Taking a much-needed break in St. Thomas.

Columbus "discovered" St. Thomas and Virgin Island during his second voyage in 1493. The Danish government signed a treaty in 1685 with the Duchy of Brandenburg allowing the Brandenburg American Company to establish a slave trading business on St. Thomas. In 1917 St. Thomas was purchased by the United States from the Danish.

But I had to take half of the medicine out of the suitcase to conserve space in the luggage.

By now all of us seemed to be getting worn out with the cruising and sightseeing. We went to a show every night from this point on. There were two shows per night. It was only January 10, about two thirds of the way through our cruising, and I was tired and out of clean clothes. The ship did not have washing machines.

Vincent and I stopped going to the exercise room. A lot of people were getting sick. The guests were coughing all over the place. We tried to stay well by not going

Was the T-shirt really worth it?

to the cafeteria. We ate in the restaurant instead. Fewer people ate there.

But the cruise wasn't over. Our next stop was St. Thomas, in the United States Virgin Islands. That was one of my favorite places to vacation because the public has access to all beaches. We couldn't get off the boat until everyone went through immigration and this long process cost us time. That seemed like a sensible process, but took forever. We were now on United States territory. The language was officially English, but Spanish and patois (a blend of Danish, Spanish, English, Portuguese, and African) was also spoken. Now that's a lot of blending.

By January 12, we were in Puerto Rico, hearing once again of Columbus. Enough already. Vincent and I took the boys to arts and crafts five minutes late and the art teacher instructing the designing of the T-shirts ignored us. The craft was to paint a white T-shirt, the theme was Brazil. When the teacher finally looked up, he said there were only XL T-shirts. We said, "OK, we'll take them. He said "not for all of you."

Here we go again. The boys were upset because they couldn't get a T-shirt and asked why they couldn't have one. A guest told me that the Asian teacher only gives the instruction once and if you're late you're on your own. This was crazy. How hard is it to paint T-shirts? It took all of one minute to explain what to do. By now other guests at arts and crafts were noticing what had happened. A lady took T-shirts out of the bag for the boys. Meanwhile, we paid full price for each boy. We didn't get a discount for children, so by rights they were entitled to T-shirts.

The other funny thing was at arts and crafts there were only 15 or 20 people that showed up for the class (out of 1,500 passengers). Now I was angry. The boys painted their T-shirts. Keeping a peaceful soul was getting harder and harder. It would have been so much easier, if they wrote in the daily program "don't bring children." I can follow rules. That would be our only class for today. I couldn't keep explaining to the boys why they couldn't participate.

Kofi and Ato took a late nap. I wanted them to go to the Fantasy Show later that night. I didn't wake them up for dinner. Most evenings they didn't eat, except for French fries. Vincent and Kwesi went to dinner without me. They ate baked Alaska for dessert. Kwesi asked me the other day if something could be cold and hot at the same time. I told him about baked Alaska. I'm glad he was able to taste it.

Columbus "discovered" Puerto Rico (which was populated by the Taino Indians) in 1493. The Spanish newcomers named the island San John Bautista in honor of St. John the Baptist. In 1809, Puerto Rico was an overseas province of Spain. In 1917, The U.S. Congress granted Puerto Ricans U.S. citizenship. In 1952, Puerto Rico adopted its own constitution by congressional decree.

Fantasy Night was a real treat for the boys and made up for the loss of activities at the arts and crafts tables. The talent was awesome. Of course the boys liked the magic show the best. Ato wanted to see the show again, so we stayed for the second show. The magician and his lovely assistant signed autographs for the boys and showed them several magic tricks

that the Kwapong boys still perform to this day. Vincent went back to the cabin with Kwesi and Kofi.

We started out training Kwesi to watch his brothers for twenty minutes at a time alone in the cabin. After about twenty minutes alone they got too loud.

Ato and I went to the Midnight Buffet. That was a challenge. Ato wanted to take pictures, but all the adults were in his way and they had no intention of moving. You think one person would see a little fellow with his camera and move aside, but that didn't happen. Pictures were taken from 11:45 to midnight. After midnight the guests were permitted to eat. Ato only ate the orange slices. I didn't do any better; I don't like a lot of odd, new, or frightening-looking foods. I had shrimp and cookies, something I recognized. Ato was still feeling seasick. Since this was our second visit to Puerto Rico, we didn't get off the ship. Also, we docked late in the night and Kofi was really sick this time.

Friday morning started off with a loud fight amongst the boys. I went next door to finish packing and each boy had a different version of what happened. We were near the end of our journey and the boys were having a meltdown. Up to that point, the boys had been behaving so well.

We went to the reception area to pick up ping pong balls and rackets. While we were waiting for an available receptionist, a man and woman walked right up in front of us and got waited on. At first, I was going to let it go, but on second thought, I said, "Excuse me, I was next."

The receptionist claimed she didn't know. She saw me with three boys in line. This happened a lot in Europe. Kind of like Columbus; now I understand why he and his crew treated the New World natives the way they did wherever they landed. It's a European thing.

So no more Mrs. Nice Guy. The boys kept asking why they couldn't go to arts and crafts. The real reason was mommy didn't want to get in a fight. I kept them away from the jewelry guy and the arts and crafts guy for a while. At lunch the jewelry guy came over to our table and showed them a trick. It was cute but he didn't want them to participate in the jewelry class. I was confused.

Saturday we disembarked in Port Everglades. We went through customs and immigration rather quickly. We had covered a total of 6,076 nautical miles. I had one hour to visit my friends in my Florida neighborhood. We caught a taxi to the airport and flew to Pittsburgh to visit family and friends about three hours later. Kofi was right, the only thing worse than being on an 18-day cruise ship is being on an 18-day-cruise ship for 18 days.

February 2006: Learning Dutch, Soccer, and Gymnastics

We returned to the Netherlands in mid-January. I started Dutch lessons and it went well initially. I understood more than ten Dutch words. The lessons were paid for by Corporate America. I also used this time as another opportunity to socialize during the cold and wet mornings. There were five students in class. Our first class was held at Sharon's house in Haren.

I was pleased when I drove to another town by myself in a stick-shift car. It was only about 30 minutes away, but I had to take the highway.

Later that week, the boys went to the dentist. I had their teeth cleaned and x-rayed in Pittsburgh. I was told that children in the Netherlands are not given x-rays for their teeth and that Dutch dentists don't give their patients painkillers for fillings. Ouch! The Dutch didn't think it was necessary to clean children's teeth and they may be right, but the Kwapong boys eat a lot of sugar. It showed at appointment time. They all had cavities. Kofi was able to get his teeth filled in Pittsburgh. Ato and Kwesi got their fillings in the Netherlands and the dentist gave them painkiller. I kept getting mixed information about the Dutch. The dentist put sealant on their teeth. It cost a small fortune but it was supposed to help prevent cavities. I started eliminating excess sugar when possible. First things first; presweetened cereal had to go.

Kofi started football (soccer) training. Ato played with Kofi's team, but he didn't like it.

"It's stupid because all the kids run for the ball at the same time," he said. He had a point. The gymnasium where the practices were held was hard to find. I followed one of Kofi's classmate's mom and still didn't know how to get there on my own. It's in the back woods. Not that kind of back woods. It was a very pretty drive. There were a lot of turns, fields, and farm land. There was a really interesting playground without dog poop. Kofi had a ball playing soccer. The coach, an older, energetic man, spoke only Dutch. The lessons were very cheap. It cost seven euros per year.

We went to a store like a Sam's Club. You needed a membership card. A Canadian friend named Cathy loaned me her card for a week while she went to Rome. We had so much fun shopping, it reminded me of home. The kids bought a ball. I bought more storage containers for toys and I still didn't have enough. Vincent bought shaving stuff. It was nice to shop in a store where you have choices, even if you chose the same old things. I went again Tuesday with another girlfriend. That's how much I enjoyed shopping there.

Monday was the last rugby practice at school. The boys earned certificates saying they completed the rugby training and what skills they had learned. The school had a celebration for the kids with cupcakes and juice.

Kwesi joined the Roldeboys soccer team. A classmate was already on the team and another one signed up with Kwesi. I thought this would be good since he would know two players. The children spoke Dutch. The coach spoke English and Dutch. Kwesi was picking up the language by playing with the Dutch children. He went every Tuesday and Thursday evening. Games would be held on Saturday. Kofi wanted to go to soccer twice a week and play competitive soccer on Kwesi's team. Kofi is one cocky and confident boy.

Rolde is a beautiful, picturesque village with lots of thatched-roof houses, trees, flowers, and an old-school windmill. Rolde was a ten-minute drive from our house. I carpooled with another parent, which was helpful. The soccer club practiced outside already and it was very cold and wet. Kwesi hung in there. He was a good, strong player. The Dutch didn't pressure you to complete the registration forms, so we took our time with them.

While Kwesi was at soccer, Kofi and Ato went to gymnastics. Gymnastics training was a bit raw and not for the faint of heart. The trainer didn't give proper instructions on how to perform a forward roll or other moves. I guess she thought they already knew how to do the moves. My boys knew how to roll from karate classes in Florida. The instructor didn't spot the kids at times. If your kid missed the bar, oh well, he would hit the floor. Ato and Kofi loved it. There was a lot of running around.

The instructor spoke English, but the class was taught mostly in Dutch. Kofi fell once and cried because he didn't understand the instructor. She spoke Dutch most of the time and sometimes forgot about the English-speaking kids. I told the boys to watch the other kids and copy the routines. I also reminded the coach that they didn't understand the rules and routines.

My American friend argued with me about why I should not expect the coach to speak in English. I thought if you advertised at an English-speaking school and took English-speaking money then you should speak Dutch and English, if you can. My girlfriend later apologized for arguing with me, I thought we were going to fight over whether or not the instructor should speak English or Dutch.

Meanwhile, the same girlfriend complained to the director of the swimming class because the swimming instructor only spoke in Dutch and was rude (by American standards) with her son. The swimming instructor would splash water in the children's faces if they didn't do their strokes correctly. She would also hit the kids on the head. This instructor went as far as to tell my friend's son that he didn't have a brain, which was why he couldn't swim. This instructor thought that the Americans' loose-fitting swim trunks were so big that they would make them drown. She only wanted boys to wear Speedos in her class.

The Kwapong boys didn't take her class; we like our baggy American swim trunks. Later I found out that it was not unusual for some Dutch teachers to make rude comments to children. Where Americans would think it was inappropriate behavior for an adult, the Dutch think it's normal. I stayed close to my boys, except Kwesi, he could use the tough-love lessons at age ten.

Around Valentine's Day, the school held a disco dance for the students. The boys each had to carry a red shirt to change into after school. The good part about parties at school was that from Year 1 and up parents didn't have to attend. The students stayed after school. When I arrived at the party, Ato and shy Kwesi were dancing. It surprised me because just that morning, they both said they were not dancing at the school's party. Peer pressure.

We made cupcakes at home with Betty Crocker icing for Valentine's Day. We found another store that sold U.S. brands.

* * *

I took Ato to the doctor for the third time. First he was vomiting and had intestinal problems. I told Vincent it was a stomach virus and it would run its course. The doctor had said it was a stomach virus. Ato was showing signs of dehydration, he was looking bad. His brothers said he looked like a ghost. His eyes were sunken into his head. I hoped the third doctor visit would be his last.

His illness was rough. He missed a lot of school. The doctor said his stomach was healing. Ato had a big knot on his ribs. The doctor said it was normal because he was so thin you can see it but it only showed on one side. He looked lopsided. That was my concern. He prescribed Zantac for the acid in his stomach.

Kwesi's classmate's father is a doctor and he said the same thing. He had worked with Ato's doctor in the past. He told me to give Ato vitamins A and D because he looked like he could be developing rickets. Rickets? So Ato and Kofi both began taking vitamins A and D. Kwesi said he didn't need it because his ribs didn't show.

Martha, my neighbor, told me to give it to all of the kids in the winter. She gave it to her children when they were little. The sales clerk at the pharmacy counter told me to give them four pills a day because of their dark skin not absorbing the little amount of sunlight available during the northern winters. Martha suggested two pills a day. There was something to be said about the lack of sun. We hadn't seen the sun in weeks.

I continued with my Dutch class. I wish I had done it sooner. It began making sense and I soon understood written Dutch better than spoken. I kept practicing with my neighbor. After Dutch class we (Cathy, Sharon, and I) went shopping in Haren, a pretty village with a lot of upscale shops and huge houses. Some houses had beautiful thatched roofs. Sharon said some shops were uppity. We didn't go in one shop because they would not let Cathy's dog Jenny come in. Couldn't Cathy tie Jenny to a pole?

"Cathy spent a lot of money in that shop and they should have dog biscuits for Jenny," Sharon said.

Sharon, who knows everything, told me that her husband got a bonus and Vincent got one also, that's why she was going shopping. Corporate America does not give the same bonus for a brother—what else is new?—but I didn't tell that to Sharon. A bonus for her husband was not the same bonus for my husband. Besides, I'm not interested in spending his money all that fast. As it turned out Vincent's bonus was disappointing to him. I think he felt down, but he wasn't the type to admit it. Who knows what he was going through or feeling? I often thought *The Secret Life of Vincent Kwapong* would be my next book.

I rushed to get back to school after shopping. It was soccer and gymnastic day. I didn't have their gym bags in the car. I drove Kwesi and Robert to soccer training. Training was cancelled. I took Robert over Ryan's house so that his mom could pick him up from Roden instead of having to drive all the way back to Assen. Ato was still slightly sick. He said his stomach hurt once in a while.

March 2006: March Madness

They say March comes in like a lion; mine started with a bang. I drove to town to buy material for the boys' costumes for an upcoming school event called World Book Day.

I was at a stop light, waiting for it to turn green to make a left turn. A truck driven by a young man, he looked like a boy, hit the car behind me and pushed it into the back of my rental car—a three-car accident.

We drove around the block where the young man worked. The lady in the second hit car, with a baby in a child car seat, called the police. The police said we didn't have to fill out a police report because we had moved the vehicles and no one was hurt. But we had to fill out the accident report for insurance purposes. My car wasn't damaged except for a very small crack around the license plate. What should have been an easy form to fill out turned out to be difficult because I could not read Dutch. The lady in the car behind me called her husband. He came from work and he translated Dutch into English and helped me fill out my form.

From what little Dutch I knew, it looked like the young man driving the truck didn't fill out his form. His boss did. The boss used his own driving information instead of the young man's license. It looked shady (but they were speaking in Dutch). Plus they were rushing to fix my cracked license plate. I told them to wait because it's a rental car. The office was cold and of course we were served coffee while we filled out the forms. I called Tami to pick up the boys from school because I was not going to make it back in time.

I found bargains in town, purchased the fabrics and then went to Tami's house and stayed an extra hour eating soup and having tea.

The next day was World Book Day. It also started with a bang. Kofi and Ato were fighting and screaming that morning over Yu-Gi-Oh cards. Those two were out of control.

At World Book Day, the students dressed up as characters from children's books. The school gave prizes for the best costumes and the boys wanted to win. They went as the Three Billy Goats Gruff. They were so cute. I made their costumes out of fake fur and they even had curly horns on their heads. The other parents at the school thought it was a great idea to make all three of them characters from the same book. But they didn't win. The judge was a Dutch bookstore owner from Assen and I don't think she got the concept of Three Billy Goats Gruff. However, the school newsletter mentioned how good the Three Billy Goats Gruff were.

It had snowed the previous night, so I thought school would be closed. No such luck. What started out as a great morning ended up with technical difficulties. One of the few times Vincent joined in on the boy's school events turned tragic—technologically tragic, that is. One of us somehow left the trunk slightly open when the boys were getting their costumes out of the trunk. As Vincent drove to work after the school event his computer dropped out the trunk. Someone found his computer and called him to pick it up. The computer was broken. We didn't know what happened or how it happened. But this was not a good time for it to happen.

I stayed out of his way and read a book. He would fall asleep on the couch instead of coming to bed. This was the routine. Once in a while I stayed up with him, but then it got stupid sleeping on the couch. Why was I staying up while he looked at the computer until he fell asleep? With his computer broken he was depressed for weeks. Vincent's life was wrapped up in that one broken computer. He was in shock that he couldn't fix his computer!

I anticipated Ato waking up at 5 a.m. and me being grumpy because it would be too early to begin a day. The snow looked as beautiful as fresh snow always looked, but I didn't look forward to driving in it with a stick shift. Being from Pittsburgh, I should be used to snow and bad weather. But I'm not. I had to pick up the boys from school in the snow.

They had an assembly the next day that continued with the World Book theme. Kofi talked a lot during the assembly, and his teacher told him to be quiet. Each class did a five-minute presentation. I drove back home without snow drama. Kofi and Kwesi were outside playing in the snow. Ato was on the computer. May tomorrow be peaceful, I thought to myself.

The next day, I missed my next Dutch class. I cleaned the house from top to bottom; it was as spotless as it was on the first day we moved in. Gwen sent an e-mail with her travel plans to Assen. I picked up Gwen and Lou and their travel friends, Mitch and Joan, from the Assen train station. We squeezed into my Ford Focus.

After a quick stop at the house I dropped them off in downtown Groningen. Gwen didn't have enough time to shop (Lou was ready to go home). I left them in Groningen with the intent of picking them up later. I picked them up at 4:30. I was late because I had to attend Kwesi's SAT meeting after school. The test sample looked hard.

Ato had a play date with John, second day in a row, so I had to invite John over this Friday. They played PlayStation nonstop. I was told European mothers don't want their kids to play video games on play dates. I didn't care. It was all socializing skills, right?

It had snowed that morning, again. The boys played soccer versus Lou and Mitch. Lou and Mitch won. The boys called them old men and were surprised that "the old men" won the game. Ato started to cheat. Vincent snuck out to buy drinks, which we had already bought; if he only would have asked, he would have known.

He waited until the last minute to accommodate guests when we knew for months they were coming to visit. He vacuumed and mopped the floors that morning, a first. I planned dinner and it turned out fantastic. Mitch cooked Argentine steaks, Gwen made mashed potatoes. I cooked large green beans that looked like giant sugar peas. Mitch sautéed the beans in a nice garlic and onion sauce. We had apple tart from Hema for dessert. Hema is the best place to buy desserts; they're large, inexpensive and they taste great.

I learned a few good cooking tips from Chef Mitch (he really was a chef). He showed me how to soften the meat. (I don't eat red meats but it's good to know for future guests).

The boys fell asleep early; yeah!!! Vincent took Mitch and Lou back to Groningen to explore the nightlife. Not all prostitutes have the luxury of a window seat; some walk the streets like in other cities. Gwen and Joan were asleep when the men came in from their scenic tour of Groningen at night. When the men got back, I stayed up late with them and talked.

Gwen and Joan enjoyed Groningen in the daytime. Mitch, Lou, and Vincent enjoyed it at nighttime. I guess the city had something for everyone.

On Wednesday, Gwen, Joan, and I went to downtown Assen, looked around a bit, and shopped some more. They missed their 12:30 train, the last one leaving Assen, so I drove them to the train station in Groningen. Gwen had relatives in Amsterdam she wanted to visit. If Vincent had told me his work schedule earlier I would have made better plans. Since he didn't and Gwen wasn't finished shopping, I asked him to pick up the boys—it was half day—and drop them off at the house. They could watch themselves until I got back.

I was in a hurry to get back to them. I saw a flash. I worried that I would get a speeding ticket. The road signs say ahead of time that a camera is coming up so slow down. I would have felt stupid to have gotten a ticket after seeing the warning clear as day. I was concentrating on not missing the Assen exit sign to get home. Oh well.

It snowed again that morning. Kwesi started acting crazy, I ignored him. He was mad at Ato over a marble. Ato, Kofi, and I played B-DAMAN, a marble shooting game that you play against others using a launcher based on Japanese anime and manga series. The faster you launch and shoot your marbles with accuracy the faster you win. I saw why Kwesi was upset; you need B-DABALLS (special marbles) to play.

* * *

Saturday was Ato's eighth birthday. I had planned to give photo albums for the kid's gift bags along with candy, and a pack of novelty stickers. My favorite store for party supplies was Wibra.

Ato was so excited he couldn't wait. Kofi just had to go to soccer training that morning, so Vincent took him. I picked up the cake and apple tart and I didn't get back home in time, so I was running a little late. I never understood the point in giving out goody bags after a party. But everyone does it, so I decided to do the same.

The party started at noon. All of Year 3 was invited, four other kids from Corporate America and my two teenage neighbors. One had a hockey game, but her sister came. She gave Ato a CD with great party music for his birthday. The boys' favorite song, "I Like Big Butts" was on it.

"Is it OK to give Ato the music CD with that song on it?" she asked. I said yes. Kwesi dressed up as a clown, but when I looked over at him, the kids were beating him up. I told them to stop beating up the clown. Other than fighting the clown, the kids were nice and so well-behaved.

But as the party came close to an end, a few boys needed to go outside and run around and let off steam. So a few kids and I played soccer. I invited a British family to come back after the party. Their daughter had to leave early to go to a horseback riding lesson. So I suggested that they could stay later and their daughter could do the fun stuff that she missed.

We made ice cream sundaes with chocolate syrup, M&M's and slagroom (whipped cream). We didn't play games. The Kwapong boys don't take losing too well, they would cry at their own party. The kids played PlayStation 2, B-DAMAN, and Legos. A few kids went upstairs, I checked on them, they said they were fine and I don't have to check up on them. OK.

Only one child cried; she accidentally got hit with a soccer ball. I told the kids that if they danced, they would get an extra gift in their bags. Each dancer reminded me about the extra gift at the end of the party.

One girl played "Happy Birthday" on the keyboard. Martha and her adult daughter, Nancy, came to the party. Martha was surprised at how big I cut the cake slices. I told her American kids eat a lot and like big cake slices. We are not modest like the Dutch. The Dutch offer cake or other goodies when you walk in their stores and homes, but I was told that it was impolite to ask for a second slice of cake. The Kwapongs always asked for a second slice of cake.

After all the kids left, the Corporate People, Martha and Nancy, stayed late. I guess the last of the lot left at 9:30 p.m. We sat around and talked about the Netherlands and politics. We talked about prostitutes; the Dutch were sensitive to the issue. They said that women were trafficked to the Netherland as sex slaves. We Americans were insensitive, maybe because of the videos in the States. The party was a great success. The children left with a photo of themselves and Ato inside of their photo albums. Thanks to my technical guy, Vincent, and modern technology, he was able to take photos at the party and print the pictures from the computer.

* * *

On the last Sunday of the month, Vincent was working in Miami. We made out just fine by ourselves. We rode our bikes downtown. Kwesi had Kofi on the back of his bike and I had Ato. His stomach was hurting again, so he couldn't ride his own bike. We went to the toy store to buy toys.

Ato received fifty euros from his birthday party. Kofi didn't have any euros, so I loaned him some plus I gave him one more for each club that he joined at school. Kofi joined the chess club, rugby club on Mondays, and soccer club on Saturday, plus he wrote a story for an extra euro. Kwesi received euros from his birthday party.

Kwesi brought Legos for 12 euros, which was fine. Kofi and Ato picked out a pack of Yu-Gi-Oh cards that cost almost 15 euros. I tried to be neutral and let them pick whatever they wanted with their

own euros. It was hard to stand by and watch, but I didn't say anything. That was where the problem started. They got home and played with the cards, but by bedtime they were crying. They had traded Yu-Gi-Oh packs earlier and Kofi wanted his pack back. Ato apparently already had the pack he bought so he wanted Kofi's pack. If they would have told me from the beginning, I could have wrapped the cards back into the box nicely and returned them, but the boxes were torn open, the way excited kids are when they get a new toy. So now, we have two extra boxes of Yu- Gi-Oh cards. I told the boys we could use the extra boxes of cards for gifts for some other kid that loved those cards, so all was not lost. That was the second time they did that.

We were almost late for school Monday morning. The time changed and I forgot to reset the clock. But we made it on time. Ato woke up about 6 a.m. instead of his usual 5 a.m. I made him lay in bed an extra 15 minutes because I thought it was an hour earlier. When he got up he was quiet and didn't wake up the other boys.

Tami suggested that we give Ato and Ivan a joint going-away party, since they were in the same Year 3 class. She also suggested that I put the extra Yu-Gi-Oh cards in the kids' party bags at Ato and Ivan's going-away party.

I went to a going-away luncheon for a Year 1 mom. I went to more parties that year than in my entire life. Someone told me with three boys and fifteen classmates each, I would attend 45 parties that school year—each child has a birthday party (not counting the going-away parties).

* * *

Vesting Bourtange was started in 1580 when Prince William of Orange ordered the building of five bastions on a sandy ridge during the beginning of the Eighty Years' War. The plan was to isolate the city from the Spanish. It was completed in 1593 under the command of Count Willem Lodewijk van Nassau.

On the last day of March (thank God the month was almost over) Kofi went on a field trip to a goat farm outside of Groningen. Kofi was quoted in the school newsletter as saying that his favorite part was milking a goat. He told me all he remembers about the field trip was trying not to step on goat poop. He wore his light-up boots and his teacher laughed. She said he would scare the goats with his flashing lights.

Year 3 Assembly was held. The theme was the Roman Empire. Ato's class was dressed in Roman togas, complete with laurel wreaths on their heads.

Ato was a Roman senator. At the assembly, we learned all about the Roman Empire, from their entertainment to the army's invasion and conquest of many lands.

Our field trip the following week was to historic Vesting (fortress) Bourtange (sandy ridges). It is in the shape of a star inside a star inside another star. The boys ran around, up, and down the ledges.Vesting Bourtange has a museum, along with a market square, restaurants, and an original cannon. Before the trip to Bourtange the boys played laser tag in Groningen.

Ato was pictured as a Roman senator on the cover of the school's April newsletter. Not to be outdone, on the back of the newsletter Kofi was pictured feeding baby goats.

Kofi, Ato, and Kwesi immersed in Greek culture.

April 2006: Greece and France

On our spring break, we decided to take another European tour. Once again, we worked up to the eleventh hour, not knowing if or when we were going on holiday. Europeans have a lot of holidays. We were faced with a two-week holiday break from school for Ascension Day, Easter and spring break. We didn't have a clue as to what to do or where to go.

I called Cherri and tried to include her in our vacation plans. It is nice at times to have a travel buddy who enjoys the art of shopping and looking around at sites without whining. Or it may be that I wanted a woman/sister's touch every now and then, without three boys crying and a husband grumbling, whew!

My sister couldn't make this last-minute trip. We tried very hard but her schedule would not allow it with such short notice.

"I do not want to be in a foreign country with just you and the boys for too long a time," I told Vincent.

Sometimes traveling isn't much fun and/or different with all men, especially not knowing the language or our destination. That's why we only stayed a short time. My mistake.

Cherri would join us in June during a one-week holiday break (more on that later). I began planning for that vacation now. Under pressure from Vincent to make a quick decision, I chose Greece, in part because we hadn't been to Greece before. I knew nothing about Greece except that a girlfriend back in the States is married to a Greek man. Well, it turned out to be a super choice with a two-day stop in Paris, France.

Our flight from Amsterdam to Paris and connecting flight to Athens was uneventful and quick. One hour from Amsterdam to Paris and three hours from Paris to Athens. The weather was warm and quite nice. We rented a car at the airport, although I was told we didn't need a car in Athens—we didn't.

Athens has a great subway system. The subway looked like a museum with beautiful mosaic art on the walls, pictures, and artifacts. As we were driving to our hotel everything literally looked Greek. We couldn't make out the signs. Usually we could put together the alphabet in another language and make out part of the words. Does Attica mean Athens?

We drove to our hotel in very heavy traffic. It took two hours to find the Ionis hotel and another 30 minutes to find a parking spot within walking distance to the hotel. Parking was a nightmare, as was driving. The traffic seemed like it was rush hour all the time. Driving was chaotic. Once we found a parking spot we left the car there as long as possible and walked, bused or took the subway.

When we finally found our hotel it was not as nice as the Internet pictures, but it wasn't bad. Most of the hotels in that area we had checked out on the Internet looked better on the Internet. The area looked a bit rough but we walked around the shopping area. It's one of the main tourist squares and it was a lot safer than it looked, even though there were women who looked like prostitutes standing on the corners, and what appeared to be a few harmless drug addicts lying on the curb.

Fortunately, the boys didn't notice those tourist attractions—yet. At least I didn't think they paid attention. Athens was a bit hectic for a family of five, but well worth the effort. We went to McDonald's

Waiting for the show!

for dinner, where the boys ate the usual. Vincent and I wanted something Greek. We noticed McDonald's had club sandwiches and chocolate pies on the menu, and a newsletter. The boys spent the rest of the evening in the hotel with Vincent. I went back out by myself to window shop. This was when I discovered my new game plan. From then on I went window shopping alone while the boys stayed in the hotel with Vincent.

On the second day of our stay in Athens, Kofi woke up feeling a bit hot. I suggested the only thing I knew to do in Athens. A friend from Dutch class said that we should go to the Acropolis. You can see it from anywhere in Athens. We ate breakfast in the hotel, which was quite good. I ate yogurt and honey with peaches. The yogurt was fresh and the coffee was very strong.

We caught the subway to Plaka Square and walked a few blocks to the tourist center to get information, since we didn't know what to do other than a field trip to the Acropolis. The tourist guy suggested that, since we had a car, we should take a one-and-a-half hour drive to Nafplio. He said that Nafplio was a pretty seaside village with a castle at the top of a hill.

That's me with Vincent and Kofi, my human backpack.

There was so much to see and do. Every time I stopped for even a minute, the boys would complain.

"You said we are going to the Acropolis and where is the Acropolis?" complained Kwesi. Ya-da-ya-da-ya-da. "You can't stop for anything but the Acropolis, we've been walking for a long time and we are not at the Acropolis." I noticed Kofi was getting tired of walking. Vincent stopped to buy Kofi a sweatshirt because he was getting cold, even though the weather was warm.

We finally made it to the Acropolis. The tickets were only six euros and free for kids. I liked Athens already, it had family-friendly prices. The Acropolis turned out to be an all-day adventure. It's a gigantic "Sacred Rock" that has archaeological treasures dating as far back as the beginning of recorded (European) time. There are about six different sites to look at.

We first went to the ancient theater of Dionysus. This was when Kofi became extremely tired. I carried Kofi on my back, because he literally couldn't walk, while Vincent took pictures. He takes better pictures than I do, plus my baby wanted to stay with his mommy.

Kwesi and Ato at the Parthenon.

The other two boys ran up, down and around the theater making up Roman and Greek war games. At this point Kofi and I sat on one of the ancient theater's surviving seats made of marble stones where the Greeks held their performances during 4th and 5th century B.C. Wow!

Our second stop was the Parthenon. I remembered building a Parthenon made of various noodles with my nephew, Jonathan, years ago. The secret to the construction of the Parthenon is that there are no straight lines. This entire site is impressive.

"Boys, you could write school reports on this field trip for years to come," I said.

Kofi and I rested again on the steps leading up to the Parthenon. He was really hot with fever and feeling weak. The other boys were having a great time. Vincent and I had to slow them down; it would not have been a good thing for them to have knocked over something that had been standing for centuries.

It was pretty crowded. School children were on a field trip and there were plenty of tourists. Vincent and I took turns sitting with Kofi. Vincent sat with Kofi while I walked quickly up to view the Parthenon with Kwesi and Ato. Vincent walked around the Parthenon with Kwesi and Ato. I carried Kofi up to the Parthenon so he could at least see the famous temple of the goddess Athena. There were about three stray dogs walking around, this was weird. As Kofi became sicker we were faced with going back to the hotel or carrying Kofi during our field trip. I chose to carry Kofi, not realizing I would be doing so for the rest of our trip in Greece.

Our next stop was the ancient city of Agora. This reminded me of the ruins of Machu Picchu, Peru, without as many mountains. Of course, to the boys it looked like a bunch of stones. Vincent stayed outside the site with Kofi and Ato. Now Ato was tired and wanted to be carried. Ato was naturally thin, but tall as me. If I carried Ato his legs would drag on the ground. So I called Vincent on our walkie-talkies to come and see this place. This was our new way to communicate during travelling with the boys. Vincent walked around the ruins carrying Kofi and Ato at the same time. What a man!

The boys wanted to know why the statues didn't have heads and were naked, I told them the statues with heads are in museums in Europe and the USA. I didn't know why the statues didn't have clothes. This one fact kept them interested for some reason.

At this point we found out that the Acropolis was much larger than we thought. The tickets were good for four days and you just might need four days to visit the entire area. Kofi was very sick and the other two were complaining about the long walks. It was a lot of walking. We had a great time. We decided this was a good place to end our field trip. The last two sites required fifteen-minute walks in two different directions, but the boys couldn't go any longer.

On our way out of the Acropolis we saw another temple. We

didn't see everything, but I saw what I wanted to see. Getting back to Plaka Square, we somehow took the long way by mistake. I asked a cop how to get back to Plaka, I wanted to buy more sweatshirts like the one Kofi had on. It was a long walk back to Plaka, which is a huge shopping square in Athens. The shops were great and the doors to the shops were open and inviting. We looked inside the shops without actually going inside, which saved us time. It felt like shopping without actually stopping so the boys didn't complain, yet.

By now I carried Kofi and Vincent had Ato on his back. Kwesi carried the camera and took pictures. I could have really enjoyed Plaka Square without my new backpack. I enjoyed the bit I did see. We were almost at our starting point when the boys spotted soccer jerseys in DSimi's store. The young man in the shop helped the boys find exactly the player's jersey they wanted. Although the boys always whined about shopping, it was OK to stop at a store if they got to pick out something. They all chose soccer jerseys with their favorite player. They were into European teams and especially UK teams, influenced from the British School.

"Do I have to play on a USA team because I'm born in the USA?" Kofi once asked me. I told him no. He said, "Good, the USA sucks in soccer."

We never did find the shop with the sweatshirt that Kofi had on. We spent quite a bit of euros in DSimi. The store clerk was very nice and friendly. We stayed longer in that shop and enjoyed our conversation with him. He had a hard time finding Kofi's small size with the player Ronaldinho's name on it. He finally brought a too big Ronaldinho shirt. Kofi said he's the best player in the world after Pelé. I was just glad they wanted something other than Legos. Ato chose the jersey of Lampard, the team captain of Manchester United. Kwesi picked an Adriano jersey.

I bought myself and a few family members T-shirts. I forgot that European sizes are smaller, or is it Americans are bigger? I couldn't fit the T-shirt when I returned to the USA. I wore it tight anyway since we lived near Miami then, where everybody wore tight clothes. Vincent bought himself some shirts. What I learned from traveling with the Kwapong boys is there are no second chances. If you see something you want, buy it then and there and hope for the best.

I was reminded by their behavior that we could only go on one field trip a day at most because they grew tired. I wanted them to enjoy traveling and remember their adventures in a pleasant way. To keep the peace, I accommodate the boys 90 percent of the time.

We ate lunch at a crepe shop Kwesi saw as we were coming into Plaka. We ate crepes from around the world. You could get just about anything in them. We took the Athens Urban Transport and then walked the rest of the way to our hotel.

After a brief rest, we asked a hotel employee for information. He said Nafplio was two hours away. Still do-able. It turned out to be a four-hour road trip, and getting out of Athens may have been two hours in itself, that was without getting lost. We had our trusty GPS and it worked great—when it was working. The drive was long but, again, worth it. I don't think you could go wrong in Greece.

* * *

We arrived in Nafplio at about 9 p.m. The shops were open and people were strolling up and down the avenues in the lively city. I later learned that it's a popular tourist location among Greeks and cruise ships.

Everything in Nafplio was either historically or naturally beautiful. We found a place to spend the night after stopping at two hotels. Our first hotel pick was way over budget. It was for the real rich and famous. We were just playing. Our second choice was good and affordable. It was late and dark; we were happy to have found a hotel on such short notice. We saw an extremely bright light on top of a hill that you could see from anywhere in town. At this point that's all we knew about the light, but we guessed it must be the castle on top of the hill. We also noticed cruise ships were docked. I don't suggest one travel into the unknown and blindly pick a city or town, but we were working on those issues.

The next day we went exploring. Nafplio is picture-perfect in every way. It is situated on the Argolic Gulf. Nafplio was the first capital of the Greek state after independence in the early 1830s.

Kwesi, me, Ato and my human backpack again.

Another interesting fact is that the first high school in Greece was built in Nafplio. Nafplio is as beautiful as a postcard, with colorful clay-like houses that have bright beautiful flowers cascading over the balconies. The gulf was blue and calm. Nafplio is a well-visited location with plenty of outdoor cafes, restaurants and shops galore.

Kofi was still hot with a fever and we were out of children's Tylenol. But we planned a field trip with sick Kofi anyway. Our field trip for that day was either a visit to a castle in the middle of the bay (Bourtzi) or a visit to the castle up on the 216-metre high hill to the fortress of Palamidi. This was the bright light we saw last night.

The boys picked the hill. They wanted to rock climb and this was the closest thing to rock climbing. There were close to 1,000 steps up to the castle, or one could drive. The boys wanted to walk the steps (except Kofi still wanted to be carried). To get to the bottom of the steps we entered a lovely shopping area that took about ten minutes to pass through. On the way I spotted a nice shop that made clay and ceramic items. I bought some very pretty blue/green coffee cups that matched my blue/green Senseo coffee pot. Senseo is popu-

lar in Europe. So, here we go again, I put Kofi on my back again and my coffee cups in my real backpack. People passing us on the steps said I would not make it to the top with Kofi. To make a long story short, I walked up about fifty steps with Kofi on my back and realized that they were right.

Vincent and Kwesi walked back to get the car and in the meantime, I found a shop with really nice jewelry and bought some silver jewelry for my mom and mom-in-law, plus silver hoop earrings for me. I had to shop quickly at every opportunity. The shop keeper was a nice English-speaking lady and she let the boys sit in a chair and take a rest. I was finished shopping by the time Vincent came back with the car. I learned a lot of short cuts during that trip.

The view while driving to the top of the castle was fantastic. Kofi still couldn't walk. We could see the entire town of Nafplio and the gulf below. The weather was nice, not hot or cold. Thank goodness, because Kofi just wanted to be held. Kofi and I found a concrete slab and sat the whole time, while Vincent and the boys explored the castle. The other two boys began running around like crazy, up and down and through the maze. School students were on a field trip. A

High above the town were the fortifications, where villagers would flee when enemies approached.

few children would take pictures of us and then I would take pictures of them taking pictures of us. We felt like the rich and famous there, also. Again we were stared at but it felt welcoming, I guess because they smiled. Kofi had a soda so he stopped complaining. An Asian family stood near us and took pictures. They pretended that they were taking pictures of themselves when they really were trying to get a picture of us. They thought we didn't know, but that was an old trick.

It was easier for us to stay at a hotel close to the airport when we had an early flight to catch. We were less likely to miss our plane. The tourist center told us to take a different route back because it was scenic and you could drive by the sea. OK, but he didn't tell us we would drive up and down mountains to see the Aegean Sea. It wasn't like driving along the coast with our hair down and blowing in the wind. Fortunately, Vincent is a great driver and can handle just about any road.

The speed limits up and down those mountains were 70, 80, and sometimes as fast as 90 mph. How can you go 90 mph around a

cliff? We saw it done. That was a scary ride.

The view was really spectacular. From the mountains we could see the Aegean Sea. The boys slept in the car, except Kwesi; we always had one man standing.

We stopped at another ruin. Archeological ruins are everywhere. We ate lunch at a tourist resort restaurant with great food. We passed lemon and orange trees in backyards. Olive groves were everywhere. We drove past really small churches about the size of mailboxes.

I wanted to know what they were. We slowed down and inside were candles, pictures and flowers. I think they were memorials.

We headed to the unknown again.

Vincent couldn't find a hotel in Athens on his trusty computer, but I remembered a Holiday Inn coming into Athens. We made it to the Holiday Inn.

While Vincent was checking us in the hotel we waited in the car. I noticed guys in identical warm-up suits. At first I thought they were on a basketball team, but not all of them were tall—not that you have to be tall, but it helps. We ordered room service and everyone was happy.

Our fourth day of the Greek trip was also Easter. To surprise the boys (they saw it earlier in the suitcase) I packed candy, Twix (Kwesi's favorite), Skittles, chocolate eggs and small Lego sets for their Easter surprise. I didn't have room in the suitcase for the little baskets. I laid all their goodies on the fake grass I packed. Kofi perked up when he saw his treats. We ate in the hotel restaurant for breakfast, good food again. While we were eating I noticed more guys in the same warm-up suits eating breakfast. I asked the hotel staff who they were. He gave the boys a picture of one of the players. He said they were famous soccer players on one of the top teams in Greece. I said I was going to ask for their autographs.

The Kwapong team meets the Greek team.

The man in the photo walked by just as we were talking about him. The hotel person asked the players for their autographs for us. The soccer players said sure and took pictures with the Kwapong boys. The man in the picture gave them his autograph. This was a really nice surprise that famous players would pause to take photos with the boys and chat with them for a while.

Later, via Internet, I found that the team was from the Athlitiki Enosi Konstantinoupoleos, the Athletic Union of Constantinople.

Then we were off to the airport to catch a flight to Paris, France. We were going to cut the trip short because Kofi was sick, but they didn't have a flight until the next day. So I said we might as well stay. Again, Mr. Vincent (I'll take full responsibility for some of this mess) and his computer couldn't find us a hotel in the entire city of Paris. I requested that we stay in walking distance of the Eiffel Tower, since I had a new backpack with legs.

Vincent put us up in the Presidential Suite of the Novotel hotel. The boys were happy as clams. They pretended that they were CEOs and presidents and took pictures of each other sitting behind the

A relic of France's long hot spring.

wooden desk, posing as if they were dignitaries.

"Kwesi, you look like the president of the United States," I said. Who knew President Obama would be in the White House several years later?

We had more room in this hotel than ever before. The lifestyle of the rich and famous didn't last more than one day. I told Vincent you can upgrade us but you can't downgrade us in the same vacation. Vincent walked around to McDonald's and bought a few things to eat. I mean a few. He came back with one 10-piece chicken nuggets for all three boys to share. He knew they could eat more than that, but Vincent said he was tired of them eating McDonald's. He ordered room service. I read my book and relaxed. All were happy until the next day, when Vincent checked us into a regular room.

I think Kofi was fine as we started our second day in Paris, but he played the "sick" card to his advantage. He did look tired. We walked the two or three blocks to the Eiffel Tower.

A series of protests had been taking place that spring, fueled by immigration and employment issues. There was evidence that Paris

Ato had his own interpretation of the Eiffel Tower.

was still burning. We took pictures of burned cars.

I wanted Kofi to see the Eiffel Tower. The older boys had seen the Eiffel Tower before, years ago when we were in Paris. At the time they were ages two and four, and I was pregnant with Kofi.

"I saw it too," Kofi said.

"How did you see the Eiffel Tower when you were in my belly?" I asked. Maybe he did, but I wanted to take him again. This time we took the lift up.

"I can't walk up," Ato said

"You walked up when you were two years old," I said.

We ate lunch in a restaurant near the top of the Eiffel Tower, took pictures, and had fun looking over the city of Paris. Kofi couldn't walk down, so he and I took the lift. The others walked down.

Ato found a 50-euro bill walking down the Eiffel Tower. Vincent checked his euros for 30 minutes or more. The boys told Vincent it wasn't his. Vincent even checked the serial numbers on his euros.

"Ato found the euro when we were walking in front of you," Kwesi said.

We took more pictures of the Eiffel Tower from the outside.

"Part of the Eiffel Tower looks like a willie," Ato said.

"Millions of people saw the Eiffel Tower and no one ever said it looked like a willie," I told Ato. There is a job for Ato somewhere. I don't know what kind of work he'll end up doing, but it scares me.

* * *

I carried Kofi back to the hotel. They wanted to go swimming later at the hotel, but the pool was closed early for a French holiday. I didn't know which holiday. I was glad it was closed, so I wouldn't have to fuss with Kofi about swimming while he's sick.

We saw an American couple dressed in their robes arguing with a French clerk because the pool closed early. They complained that the pool should be open every day because it's an international hotel. The boys thought it was funny that the man was screaming about a closed pool on a holiday.

I believe most people would choose to visit the world-famous Louvre Museum in Paris, but the Kwapong boys would have argued and whined for days if they had to see the Mona Lisa; they're not that interested in her.

A view of the Seine.

"Why does she look like a man?" they would have screamed. Plus, I don't think I would have made it far with Kofi on my back.

Instead, I surprised them with a field trip to the Cité des Sciences et de l'Industrie museum Star Wars Expo. And yes, the boys loved it! When we got in line to buy our tickets, they asked, "What does Star Wars mean in French?"

I pretended I didn't know. They were so excited to see all the Star Wars memorabilia from the movie. Kofi perked up when he saw the Star Wars sign. He was selective about when he could walk and when he couldn't walk. Suddenly he could walk. The museum was wonderful and had a lot more to see in addition to the exhibit, but that was all the Kwapong boys could handle in a day. We had our Star Wars map and followed it entirely through every exhibit starting with number one. Our favorite—who else? Exhibit No. 6, Darth Vader.

We stopped at a McDonald's, but I had trouble ordering food in English since I couldn't speak French. I even tried pointing to the pictures on the wall and this was just as difficult. A man standing in line spoke English and French and he offered to help us order our food. Kwesi is currently taking French in high school. I hope he passes with flying colors.

Back at the hotel the boys went swimming. It cost seven euros for adults to go swimming. I didn't want to swim anyway, so I just watched the boys. They had to wear swimming caps because it's a French law. A few chairs over, a couple were kissing as if they were at home. I guess that's where French kissing came from.

Later that evening, Mr. Day Late and a Dollar Short suggested a boat ride along the Seine River. He comes up with suggestions at the oddest time. We were sooooo tired but we went anyway, after all this was our last day in Paris. The boys fell asleep during the canal ride because it was late. The canal ride was interesting and we learned some facts about the buildings we passed. It was getting dark, but the good news was we waited another 10 or 15 minutes and watched the Eiffel Tower light up, like New Year's Eve. I'm told it does this every hour on the hour after 9 p.m. That was exciting and worth waiting for. The boys woke up to watch the lights. Then we drank hot chocolate and walked back to the hotel with two boys on our backs.

The next day, we held up the line going through the airport, all because the French insisted that the boys remove their pant belts by themselves without help from us. Do you know how long it takes for three boys to remove their belts in an airport? The people waiting in back of us were not happy and one man tried to pass over them but Vincent stopped him.

Some of those Europeans could be so rude.

* * *

We had to go back to the Netherlands in time for school. Last term we took the kids out an extra few days and Kwesi got an N in history. His teacher and the school wouldn't let Kwesi start an assignment late. Because he didn't get the assignment on the first day it was given out, he didn't have to do it. In the States they let you make up work that you missed even if you are on holiday.

Things soon settled back to normal—too normal. For example,

Ato and Kofi had a big fight over Yu-Gi-Oh cards, again. One boy bent the other boy's card. Vincent was late coming home from work to watch them, so I took them along to Kwesi's Year 6 meeting late. When we arrived at the school the meeting had ended. I got the information for the Year 6 meeting about an end-of-term field trip to England. Kwesi needed a sleeping bag and a waterproof coat. We had the rest of the items on the list. I started packing his suitcase because I didn't want to wait until the last minute. I paid for half of the trip that same day.

I changed my walking schedule with Tami to 10:30 a.m. instead of 8:30 a.m., which I thought would work out better because I could write/type in my journal and start my book. I planned to dedicate a minimum of two hours in the morning to the project before I went walking. I intended to write before housework and see if I could make progress this way. Otherwise I'd just be a struggling writer.

Saturday was a national holiday. Vincent was in the States for business. Kofi and I rode our bikes to spring soccer training held around the corner from our house. The field was closed due to Queen's Day. It would be the Queen of the Netherlands' birthday tomorrow, but the celebration started Saturday. Orange is the national color of the Netherlands, so we wore something orange.

"Why does the queen have to have a birthday?" Kofi asked. He didn't want to miss soccer, particularly since he had on his new jersey with Ronaldinho on the back. Kofi was whining loud and long. It took me a while to make him stop.

I drove the boys to the center of town instead of cycling because it was cold. I wanted to take a look around and see what went on during Queen's Day. People put out old items for sale like a flea market. We didn't see anything we wanted to buy. We stopped at the toy store and the boys bought two small boxes of inexpensive Legos.

After shopping we ate dinner at a local Chinese restaurant. The boys ate sweet and sour chicken instead of their favorite, General Tso's chicken and spring rolls. These Chinese dishes are the only things they'll eat other than McDonald's. I talked them out of the soda which cost half the bill, and told them I'd buy a big one. The grocery stores were closed (who knew?) for Queen's Day. I took them home because they didn't want to look for a store that was open. They wanted to open their Legos. I rode my bike alone back into town and found one store open and bought their sodas.

One of the American families invited us over for a Queen's Day cookout. We wore something orange just in case.

The boys were excited about going over to Donnie's for the cookout. It was cold and gray as usual. I packed extra sweaters along with jackets in case it rained. We ate and stayed indoors due to the weather. Donnie's mother was a really good cook and hostess. Their son hogged the X-box. It was set for two players. My three boys rotated while Donnie stayed on one controller. I asked him to play fair and put the X-box on four players. But the excuse Donnie used was that he was the only one who knew how to play the game. I told him that as much PlayStation 2 as the Kwapong boys played, they were fast learners.

After a great dinner, everyone walked to the town center in Haren, about a three-minute walk, for the carnival in celebration of Queen's Day. Donnie's father bought all the ride tickets (thanks) at a booth. The kids wanted to go on the bumper cars. When the bell rang for the kids to get off, you had to run and grab a car before someone else got to it. There wasn't a waiting line. Donnie's father then found out that you had to buy bumper car tickets for the bumper cars. You then put the tickets in the car to start the cars.

It took us three tries before we finally got a car for one set of kids, two to a car. By this time we were good at getting cars. Between me, the other American family and the Canadian family running for cars we finally got all the kids into cars. I told Ato and Kofi to stay in the car when the bell rings and they could ride again and again. Ato said someone pushed him out of the car and he hit his head. He cried.

The Dutch kids are tough and unruly at times, just like American kids. You could stay in a bumper car as long as you kept putting tickets in it. Most of the people didn't get out of their cars. I saw a few teenagers smoking cigarettes in the bumper car while they were getting bumped. I saw a teenager talking on a cell phone in a bumper car. There may have been only two or three open cars after each bell. The race to an open car was fierce. I rode in a bumper car with Kofi, it was a rough ride. I was screaming and the American and the Canadian families looked a bit embarrassed, maybe they were just concerned. Every time we passed them they would ask me if I was OK. I'm not one for rides.

The younger kids wanted to go on a different ride. That's when we found out that each ride had its own ticket booth and you couldn't exchange them for a different ride. At this point Donnie's father asked for his money back, and they gave it to him so that the kids could ride different rides.

We played games and won a few prizes. Everyone walked back to the house except the Kwapong boys. Ato played a game and some Dutch kids pushed the machine so that the prize tokens would fall out and Ato got extra prize tokens. Ato took a long, long time to make a decision over a toy prize. Donnie stayed with us to show us how to get back to his house (but I remembered it was only a three-minute walk) without getting lost. We ate delicious homemade desserts and ended our evening drinking coffee, of course.

May 2006: Flowers!

Monday the boys started hockey. Again the two older boys grumbled after the game because, according to them, Mr. Underhill made the teams uneven and it wasn't fair. I told them a lot of the world is unfair and they would have many crying days ahead because of unfairness.

Kofi, the youngest, was doing just fine. He was on the winning team!

The next day, May 2, was beautiful and sunny, a rare day in the Netherlands. I went to Dutch lessons. This was my second session. I struggled, but continued to give it an extra effort - I should have gone for Spanish since I would be back in Florida soon. The Connect Company that helped with our move to the Netherlands advised me to tell the doctors, dentist, school (which I have done already) etc., etc. that we are moving at the end of July.

Tomorrow was supposed to be even nicer. Spring is a great time to be in the Netherlands; the days are long, really long. It gets dark between 10 and 10:30 p.m. It was hard getting the boys to sleep. Kofi thought it was still afternoon at bedtime because it was so bright outside.

Wednesday brought with it another school half day. Tami organized a Year 3 boys outing at Sprookjeshof. That's an attraction park with a bunch of play rides that you push, pull, etc. all powered by hands and/or feet. Think of it as an amusement park that uses your own energy—Flintstones style. There's a storybook land with puppets. It looked like fun for the kids and the price was right.

Another sunny day, so it appeared to be official summer weather. The boys were at the age where they could run off by themselves. I sat in one spot and read magazines.

* * *

Ato's after-school art club would start in three weeks. The real queen, my sister Cherri (there's one in every family) had a birthday coming up soon. She wouldn't be wearing orange, then again, she might. I was never good at buying presents before the day of the event, now I have an excuse. I'm in the Netherlands and she is in Pittsburgh, yahoo!

On Saturday, Kofi was invited to a party at Hof van Saksen, my favorite place for kids' parties. It's fun and cost-friendly. The other boys went as well. I felt like the American on that Oprah show in which Europeans complained that American women dress in drab fashions. All the English women had on high-heeled sandals and dresses, or at least cute flat sandals with bubbles and other extreme decorations on their shoes. The Asian woman had on high-heeled sandals and smart-looking pants. The Germans were dressed a bit more casual but cute. I, the only American, wore my lavender nylon track suit with a jacket wrapped around my waist and sneakers. It was a party for six-year-olds, for Pete's sake! Most of the foreign (or am I the foreigner?) women wore makeup. I made a note to tell Tami on our next walk that we have to step up our game so that we can represent American women better. I decided to wear my heels and makeup to the school play Tuesday. How about that!

Kwesi was invited to a party at Hof van Saksen. It was the second time that week going to the same place. I painted my toes for that party. The other two boys went as well (of course). It was big enough that Kwesi could go with his schoolmates and the other two could play in a different area/room and never come in contact with Kwesi's party mates. I paid their entrance fee of two euros each. I would be back there yet again next Saturday with Ato, who was invited to a party. Kwesi laid his card for his classmate on the table next to the gifts (he said the gift table was full). If Kwesi wasn't so shy he would have handed it to the girl. She couldn't find her card with her euros in it. The good news was I could replace it (11 euros).

* * *

Ato chose to go to the after-school club along with his fellow gymnastics partners instead of to gymnastics. Kofi went to gymnastics by himself. Kofi is one self-motivated kid. He didn't care that he was the only English-speaking kid in class. He had fun. I had to juggle picking up Ato from school and going back to get Kofi at the same time because Tami's boys were sick. She had planned to take one to gymnastics with Kofi and I was supposed to pick up her son and Ato from art class. Somehow it worked out well. Kwesi went home.

Ato was in "Stoppit," the school play, that night. His teacher wrote the play. Ato is such a good actor. He speaks loudly and confidently. Moments like those are when parenting is a real joy.

I love the school events in the Netherlands. In the USA, our PTA sold sodas. There, the PTA sold wine and beer. Maybe that's why so many dads attended PTA meetings in the Netherlands. I didn't have wine because I was the designated driver for the evening. I started to tape the play and soon ran out of film. That's when I needed my technical advisor (Vincent), who was still in Miami. After I learn how to book trips, I'll tackle the camera. A stay-at-home mom has so much to learn.

On Wednesday morning I took a splinter out of Ato's hand in front of the school. We were in the car and he was screaming his head off. I looked up to see if the other parents were looking. I got the splinter out and put a bandage on it.

I appointed myself travel director for the Kwapong family, and went to a travel agent in town. We wanted to travel to Greece again with Cherri. No luck on a Santorini trip. The travel agent only had eight-day trips. We only wanted to go for four days. She suggested we fly into Crete and take a ferry to Santorini, but she didn't have packages for that. The Internet hadn't worked for two days. I felt good about planning our vacation early—early for us.

Kofi was invited to Molly's for a play date. I found him standing in the school yard whining. He couldn't decide if he wanted to go over Molly's or Ivan's. Ivan was having the Year 3 boys over for a waterslide day. Kwesi was angry; he didn't want to go and he said he couldn't watch himself for three hours. Molly's mom decided to crash the party (Tami didn't mind) and met Kofi over at Ivan's house. Kofi could go to Molly's on Thursday. Molly had a dog that Kofi enjoyed playing with. It turned out that the waterslide was so much fun, Kwesi joined in the fun after he pouted for an hour. Tami made lunch for everyone and we ate ice cream.

* * *

On Thursday, the Year 3 class went on a field trip to the Drent Museum in Assen. Ato was supposed to bring a daypack to put his snack in. I thought it said paper bag and he was the only kid carrying his snack in a bag (everyone else had a small daypack) and his bag was already ripped. I saw him in line this morning to catch the school bus.

I was hoping that Ato's friend would carry Ato's snack in his daypack. I would think the teacher would tell him to do that, but probably not here in the Netherlands. It's every man, woman and child for himself/herself.

Now, for the first time, I felt I was ready to go back to the States, partly because our time in the Netherlands was coming to an end. It was difficult to maintain two separate households. The landscaper in Florida left our yard with a big hole in it, where he had removed several dead trees. Vincent called him and the landscaper said "I thought I had until July to finish it, that's when she said she'll be back." If he waited until July we would have fines from the home-owners association. The yard looked like a hurricane hit it, and it wasn't hurricane season yet. The landscaper finally put the palm trees in the yard. Vincent sent me the pictures.

The weather in the Netherlands was so bright and sunny that I couldn't remember the cold, gray weather. It changed so suddenly.

Kwesi was taking a standardized test. Ato said his field trip to the museum was nice and he had put his snack in his pocket. He didn't have to carry it around all day. Ato was at a play date with his friend John. Kofi was at a play date with his friend Joey. Kofi was sup-posed to go over to Molly's today, but he chose Ms. Jenkins, Joey's pretty mom, over six-year-old Molly. I told you earlier that Kofi likes older women.

I was left alone again with Kwesi, but this time I told him to grab a kid from the parking lot in front of the school. He picked Norman, partly because he was the only kid standing in the school yard at the time. Kwesi had Norman over for a play date. That was a bit differ-ent. The boy watched TV and sucked his thumb the whole time; he was in Year 6 with Kwesi.

I took Norman home; his mom gave me a big bowl of jollof rice, an African dish, and shrimp, so I wasn't complaining. Then I picked up Ato, who was sick with allergies. He fell asleep at John's house, so John's mom was worried. I didn't want to tell her the boys slept every day from 6 to 8 p.m. because they wake up at 5 a.m.

The Kwapong boys were really excited about Vincent coming back from Florida. They e-mailed him and called him every day be-cause he said he was bringing back three Pokémon Game Boy games called Emerald, Sapphire, and Ruby. Later in the States, a young man at GameStop told me Emerald, Sapphire and Ruby were the same Pokémon games with different characters. What a waste of money. I tried to get them to buy one Pokémon game and share, but it didn't work. Ato had 100 euros to pay for his brother's games. Ato threatened the other boys by warning them that if they didn't coop-erate with him, he would not buy them the games. Maybe I'll think of some other payment for the games when Vincent comes home. Kofi was the only one who deserved a gift; his grades were fantas-tic!

The last day of testing for Kwesi ended that week. It was another sunny day. Kwesi wanted a gift at the end of testing because I gave Ato a book for his spectacular performance in the school play. Kofi wanted a gift because he was in the chess club, gymnastics, rugby, hockey, soccer and he made the best grades.

My morning walk with Tami included her guest from Houston. Sonny was a friendly fellow who talked with a southern drawl. It was kind of nice to hear a familiar accent in a faraway land. My roots are in Alabama and Mississippi.

* * *

Sunday, May 13, was a perfect day. I waited all weekend to open Kofi's Mother's Day gift that he made for me at school. He had tried to get me to open it earlier, but his teacher sent a note asking the moms to wait until Sunday. Kofi opened my present for me. "You're taking too long," he said. It was a spectacular painting of bright yel-low sunflowers, better than van Gogh's painting of sunflowers. The weather was a fine cool day with a hint of sunshine. Sounds like a drink.

Mother's Day (Moeder Dag in the Netherlands), was spent at the Keukenhof. I stood in front of the mirror admiring my hair. Ato asked, "what are you doing?" I told him that I had taken my braids out and had a new hairstyle.

"What is it?" he asked.

"It's called a modified afro."

"It doesn't look like an afro and it doesn't look modified," he said, and then walked away. I wore my gray afro out anyway.

Our family and friends among the flowers.

This would be my second try at going to the Keukenhof. The boys didn't protest this time. Kofi said, "What are we going to do at the Coconut?" Kofi called the Keukenhof the Coconut all day, due to the way I pronounced it.

The Keukenhof is a beautiful spring park most noted for its stunning tulips. In the 15th century the Keukenhof was owned by Jacoba van Beieren, the Duchess of Holland, Zeeland and Henegouwen between 1417 and 1433. Her estate grounds were used for hunting and gathering herbs for the kitchen at the castle. Keukenhof literally means "Kitchen Garden."

We met Thelma Smith, Vincent's colleague, with her husband, Nate, and their two girls at McDonald's. They enjoyed breakfast while we ordered take-out lunch. They are late risers compared to our early 5 a.m. rise-and-shine habits.

While having a brilliant conversation at McDonald's, we suddenly realized why Europeans dislike the Americans. Our theory is it was because Americans can buy a hamburger for $1. The Smiths visited England years ago and said a hamburger cost £17. Throughout Europe a burger is more expensive than a USA burger. It's not American politics that Europeans dislike at all. It boils down to the $1 burger.

The Smiths followed us by car to the Keukenhof. The drive was uneventful except for a traffic jam near Amsterdam due to construction and a car accident. When we arrived I was excited and thrilled. Martha Stewart had a show featuring the Keukenhof years ago. I think the Keukenhof named a tulip for her—don't quote me on that information. It is an amazing show of flowers bursting with color. I saw every color tulip, and color combination, imaginable. Some even looked like roses. Among the tulips were other flowers such as iris, narcissus, and some I had never heard of like

The first spring flower show was in 1949. There was a tulip craze during the 17th century. In 1637 the tulip market collapsed, ruining thousands of people who had sold their businesses and family jewels to trade tulip bulbs.

puschkinia. There were so many flowers I didn't know where to turn first. Each was more impressive than the next.

The Keukenhof was hosting its 57th exhibition. There were many different garden styles. I don't think we saw them all, but we saw most of them. There were also pavilions with exhibitions. I went inside the gorgeous orchid exhibit and the smell reminded me of a funeral parlor. My favorite tulip by far was the Bermuda—or was it Barbados? It had jagged leaves in the form of a tulip and was deep red in color. I would have loved to stay longer, and I can see why one would go to the Keukenhof year after year.

I could have found a bench and reflected on life, but the children weren't having it. We tried following the map, but soon gave up on that idea. The children wanted to go to the children's section.

I thought we should let them have fun first. Thelma and Vincent thought the kids should go last because they would be tired. We went to the children's section somewhere in the middle of the trip. The children thought the playground was the best ever. The garden maze was amazing. Vincent and I got lost and it wasn't that big. The

children wanted to play hide and seek but we told them not to run around in it and disturb other visitors. The children went inside a windmill, climbed to the top and looked out over the balcony. The Japanese country garden was next. This garden had mostly shrubs and trees of various shades of green, but not many flowers. It was equally as stunning. There were many different gardens, each with their own theme. Scattered throughout the park were amazing bronze statues by famous artists. The children thought the naked statues were the funniest. They missed the point, or maybe I missed the point. Is a naked statue funny?

The best part of the park for the children was running on pads in a pool of water. From a distance it really looked like they were running on water. Kofi fell in the pond. Kofi said Kwesi pushed him in. Kwesi said he didn't. We had planned to end our day at the Keukenhof, so it didn't matter much. Actually, the Keukenhof ended us because it was closing. The gates would be locked if we didn't get our cars out by closing time. Our cycle continued at McDonald's again for dinner. We got back to Assen at midnight.

* * *

Monday was the beginning of "Nederlandse Week" at the British School, which meant students and staff would be focused on Dutch that week. On Tuesday Kwesi and Ato went on a field trip to Vesting Bourtange.

Kofi went on a field trip to Orvelte in Belevenis. According to the school's paper, Orvelte is one of the five most beautiful Dutch villages and depicts what life was like for the people who live in the local area both nowadays and in days gone by. The children saw old Saksische Boerderijen (Dutch farms), the cheese factory, the clog maker, the ironsmith and more exciting old professions. I would like to have seen that myself. The weather looked bad, as if it were going to rain any minute.

* * *

Wednesday I went to pay the dentist's bill. I was told that everything is paid through the bank. The dentist did not use credit cards or cash. That was common in the Netherlands. I had been putting off paying the bill. One, I thought Vincent took care of it (he didn't), and two, Vincent's name was on the debit card, not mine. The dentist had a steep late fee (159 euros twice), but no complaints from me because I was late paying it. We had so many bills the man at the dentist office called his bill-paying office to clear up exactly what we owed. We had double and triple of some of the same bills. No wonder the late fees were so high.

On Saturday it rained. I asked Kofi if he wanted to go to soccer training; he said no. I was prepared to sit in the rain with a cup of coffee while he played. I guess Kofi is a fair-weather American kid.

Thelma and her girls called us to meet them at an indoor play place in Groningen, but Kwesi had a party to go to and a sleepover afterwards. Instead, Thelma drove to Assen with her girls to visit us. We went to Hof van Saksen so that I would be close enough to Kwesi's party to get him there on time. I got him to the party on time. It was at a movie theater and the birthday boy and his parents were late for their own party. They offered me cake, which I took to go. I'm training myself to "just say no," but, so far I was not having any luck. I gained a good 10 lbs. That was Kwesi's first sleepover at a friend's house. After a delightful day, we went back to my house, where I cooked dinner with Thelma's help.

"I can cook for thirty people, but not for small groups," Thelma said. We cooked Argentine beef and roasted chicken legs which were pre-seasoned from the store. All I had to do was put them in the oven. We also had mashed potatoes, string beans, and apple tart and ice cream for dessert. Together we did great.

Nate joined us later in the evening and we talked for hours. We planned a trip to Belgium, during Ascension Day because it is a Dutch holiday. Nate wanted to visit some trenches from World War I. I asked him if that was where trench coats originated (Yes). Nate is a history buff.

Lynette, their four-year-old daughter, had asthma and wasn't feeling well. We had planned to go to the Emmen Zoo Sunday, but Thelma called that morning and said she had taken Lynette to the hospital. The first time Thelma took Lynette to the hospital they said it wasn't critical and they sent her home. A few hours later their little girl was not feeling any better. Thelma took her back to the hospital and this time the hospital gave her a nebulizer for her asthma.

Health care in the Netherlands is interesting. Everyone has health insurance and, I was told several times that the Dutch believe the body can heal itself. In some cases it can and others, oh well, you are out of luck.

The weather was gray and looked like it was going to rain buckets, but it never did. We stayed home thinking that the weather was too bad to go to the zoo. One really shouldn't cancel a plan due to the weather. One just needs a plan B.

Speaking of plan B, Vincent and I really worked at planning a trip to Santorini, Greece, and Venice, Italy. These were the two places my sister, Cherri, wanted to visit. She even had a particular place in Amsterdam that she wanted to visit. I had to ask my Dutch neighbor about it. My holiday planning wasn't going so well. The Dutch plan their holidays months in advance, sometimes a year in advance, not like Americans who plan a two- or three-day vacation on the spur of the moment. The travel agent told me that it was unheard of to visit a place for three or four days and with such short notice. My neighbor couldn't believe that I wanted to go to Greece for four days instead of two or more weeks.

June 2006: Cherri Returns

Vincent, the boys and I drove to Schiphol Airport in Amsterdam to pick up Cherri. We went straight to Albert Cupyt Market, just as we did the first time Cherri visited us. We walked the entire length of the outdoor market and back up again. The boys were uninterested and sauntered back to the car and waited. We would have looked at every stall but a Dutch woman on a bike said that Magna Plaza was more upscale. The boys were hungry. We looked for a McDonald's and saw a Kentucky Fried Chicken (KFC) a few doors down from McDonald's and voted on KFC. It's been a year since I ate at KFC. I loved it, but KFC didn't have biscuits.

We toured the Rijksmuseum, the largest museum in the Netherlands. The Rikjsmuseum has exhibits by Rembrandt, Vermeer, and other great Dutch Masters. Ato and Kofi were ready to leave as soon as we entered the museum. Kofi pointed at one of the great works of art and said, "Look at his naked butt." The boys laughed. I found a bench for Ato and Kofi to sit quietly. They pulled out their Game Boys and entertained themselves. The rest of us toured the museum.

Cherri commented on how much Kwesi knew about art. Their school taught them about van Gogh, Rembrandt, and other Dutch

Kwesi shows off for Aunt Cherri.

artists. It was Rembrandt's 400th anniversary. What captured our attention was a portrait by Jan Mostaert of an African, painted between 1475 and 1556. What was unique is that it was the only portrait of a black man during the Renaissance that we found. Not much is known about the man's identity in the painting but it was believed that due to his rich clothing he was someone of importance.

I left my tourist information book at home, so I called our friend Nate for information on what else to do. Nate gave us step-by-step instructions on where to go and how to get there. It worked out quite well. He directed us to the Jourtaan area. All three boys were sleeping in the back of the car. We weren't sure what streets; when we found one it was on a one-way street. Vincent drove around the same block three times looking for parking. At this point I said, "Let's go home." It felt like the movie *Groundhog Day.*

We drove back to Assen. I walked to our neighbors to ask the teenagers to babysit the boys. They jumped up and down in excitement. The girls were saving their money for something special. At 9:30 p.m. we drove to Groningen to a coffee house to listen to Nate

147

play drums in a jazz band. We met and chatted with the band members and ended our evening around midnight.

* * *

The next day, I gave Vincent instructions to pick up the boys after school and take them to gymnastics. Mama and Cherri were going on a field trip to Utrecht with Cynthia, who arrived late. We missed the train to Utrecht by mere minutes. We caught the next train about twenty minutes later.

Utrecht is the fourth largest city in the Netherlands. I thought they served coffee on the train but I was wrong. Cherri packed fruit, bagels, and apple tarts that we ate on the train. We were laughing and talking until a Dutch man sitting across the aisle from me said, "This is the quiet train and I am enjoying it." OK, so in other words shut the beep up. "Holland is a funny country," the Dutch man said.

It sure is. I can smoke marijuana in a public park but can't laugh on a train. This was one of the few times I wrote in my journal and experienced the Netherlands at the same time. As I looked out of the window I saw miles of green trees and farm land with sheep. I told Cynthia we'll use made-up sign language. Put up one finger if you want to laugh. Two fingers mean it's not funny. The terrain is flat and grassy. The weather was cold and gray. A threat of rain was possible any minute. I was relaxing on the train; the cows and horses were relaxing in the fields. For our next train trip we'll upgrade to first class so that we can have our own private booth.

* * *

Sunday, Cherri and Vincent spent all day on the Internet searching for ways to visit Venice, Italy, and Greece. It wasn't possible. The week the boys were out of school was booked solid. However, we were finally able to piece together a tour.

A week later, we were off—almost. Cherri and I were packed and ready, but we had to patiently wait for Vincent to finish up with work. When he was finally ready, we hit the road. We didn't stop in Germany but enjoyed the lovely drive through Germany's countryside, with castles dotting the mountainside every so often.

Innocents abroad—Vincent, Cherri and the boys in Basel.

Our first stopover was in Switzerland. We arrived in Basel, Switzerland, about six hours after starting out. We ate in the beautiful, contemporary Ramada Plaza, and then went directly to bed. Basel borders on both Germany and France. How cool is that? I recalled that every year the Miami Museum of Modern Art hosts an exhibit based on the annual Basel art festival.

After a good night's rest, we looked for a restaurant to eat breakfast. It was late for breakfast and the boys were complaining. Kofi said, "I can eat a donut." As we were strolling and looking for a place to eat we passed a McDonald's. McDonald's won again. It was easy, it was the same, and the boys enjoyed it every time. Vincent didn't want McDonald's, neither did I, but our time was limited.

After the boys ate their late breakfast, we went for a walk through downtown Basel. It was gorgeous. The northern part of the Rhine River ran through the city. We sat on concrete steps that bordered the river edge and watched a few people with their feet dangling in the river. Kofi took off his shoes and put his feet in the river. We all

The Rhine, as it makes its way through Basel.

hoped he wouldn't wade in too deep and fall into the river. After a few minutes the other two boys took off their shoes. I told Cherri that it was a good time to escape and go window shopping.

With walkie-talkies in hand, Cherri and I walked up a slight hill to the shops. This plan worked out great. The weather was nice and there were plenty of shops to see. It was a holiday in Basel, so the market was closed, but the shops were open. We were joined later by Vincent and the boys. We visited one tourist attraction, only because we passed it on the way to the shops. It was a church with fresco walls and a famous statue. We took pictures and moved on. We all agreed that we would love to visit Basel again.

It was time to go to Italy. Our drive to Milan was uneventful. The weather was a bit drab. We got a few rain showers as we headed toward Zurich, Switzerland. We stopped there, just to say we had visited the city. Zurich looked like your typical big city. But then again, we just drove through and made one stop, so I could be wrong.

With the European-style buildings and the soft, falling rain, it was still an enjoyable visit. I don't think one could go wrong in Europe because the cities are hundreds of years old. It seemed that every city was a good choice.

We reached Milan at night. I chose Milan because we had not been there. We had already seen Venice, and it's good to venture to an unknown city. Plus I thought Milan would have unique styles that Cherri would enjoy because fashion and design are her passions. We stayed at the Hilton Milan; it had that sleek Italian design, really HGTV-ish.

Milan is the second largest city in Italy. It's a fashion and design capital as well as a major E.U. financial and business center. The hotel clerk insisted that we take the subway. He said parking was very hard to find in Milan even on a Sunday.

The profusion of art made Italy a gem.

What I didn't know was that the shops are closed on Sunday. Sunday shopping in the States is taken for granted, but many Europeans shops are closed on Sunday and open late on Mondays. That changed our plans a bit. Instead of shopping, we ate breakfast at a lovely Italian restaurant. The first restaurant we saw when we got off the subway was a good enough choice for us. Cherri ordered coffee, but she didn't like the strong taste. Kwesi ate pizza.

As soon as we got off the subway we saw this ginormous white gothic-style cathedral, Duomo de Milano. It looked like it was being renovated.

It was located in the center of the town square and is one of the largest cathedrals in the world. The cathedral took 500-plus years to build, beginning in 1386.

After breakfast we visited Castello Sforzesco; behind the castle was a large park. The Castello Sforzesco once was the home of the Sforzas, the ruling family of Milan. The original construction began in the 14th century. Francesco Sforza reconstructed the castle in

Not that everyone appreciated the art!

1450. The castle was damaged during World War II, and now it is home to several museums. We walked around the courtyard of the castle.

Vincent purchased a soccer ball and played soccer with the boys in the park. The park had many visitors, many of whom were playing soccer as well. Milan has two soccer teams. Cherri and I walked back to the shopping area near the Duomo de Milano where we found a mall that was open and spent a short time shopping.

Vincent and the boys met us at the shops. The part of Milan that I saw featured a lot of what looked like ancient buildings with Roman/Greek architecture. The buildings were close together. We didn't have a lot of time to really explore Milan and since it was Sunday, it wasn't the best day for shopping. However, we loved what we saw. What was nice about Milan and Europe is that it was new to us. Just being there in Milan and looking around at the different places and people was a treat in itself.

* * *

Sunday evening, I volunteered to drive to give Vincent a break on our way to Preganziol, Italy. The drive was absolutely beautiful. The weather was clear and sunny. We passed white houses with red clay tile roofs located on rolling hills. There was little traffic going in our direction, but the opposite side of the road was backed up with heavy traffic which was barely moving. The boys napped or played with their Game Boys. Vincent slept also, and missed the scenery

We spent the night in Preganziol. It was late when we arrived, so we checked in to a hotel while the boys played with rocks in the parking lot. Kids can make up a game out of anything. They were collecting rocks for their rock collection. After we put our luggage in the hotel, we drove to a nearby restaurant. It seemed to be crowded, but we were seated quickly. No English there, but we managed to order the usual pizza for Kwesi.

I looked across the room at other people's plates; my plan was to point to something I wanted to eat instead of speaking English.

So after we struggled with the Italian waitress—or the Italian waitress struggled with us—we waited until an English-speaking waiter came with an English menu. I noticed that Italians ate a whole pizza pie per person. It was served whole, not cut into triangles, and eaten with a fork instead of your hands. Old habits are hard

Cherri, the shopping queen.

to break. I still picked the pizza up with my hands. Cherri ordered lasagna and said it was the best ever. The food was excellent, as always, in Italy. I think it's the fresh ingredients. After dinner we drove back to the hotel and got ready for our day trip to Venice.

* * *

We couldn't have asked for clearer skies and milder temperatures for our drive to Venice. On the way, we looked at the villas and dreamed about buying one for our visit back.

After about 20 minutes, we got a bit lost and ended up where the cruise ships docked. When we turned around, we missed our turn for parking and had to drive about eight minutes out of Venice. We decided to take the first parking sign we saw instead of driving another 10 or so minutes to get back to the water bus that takes you to Venice.

The great thing about traveling is you can visit the same place twice and the experience is quite different. This time we went into Venice "backward" on a small boat. We bought tickets for a boat

Even the alleys in Venice are paved with water.

ride that leaves for Venice and returns to the parking lot every hour. It was our second trip to Venice and Cherri's first. Venice is a shopper's paradise. I thought I was equipped for this but it turned out I was not in the same league as my sister. We walked/shopped and walked/shopped and walked/shopped some more. I grew up with her, yet I'm amazed at her shopping abilities.

Not everyone can achieve such a high level of shopping commitment. I surrendered my shopping to a Higher Power.

I told Vincent to take the boys to Burger King and that we would meet them in an hour and a half. That was the only landmark I remembered from our last trip. After shopping with Cherri, we met the boys at Burger King. Several shops were closed because they opened late on Mondays, a European thing.

"My feet are burning on the bottom!" Kofi whined. That was our sign to make our way back to catch the boat. We noticed that most of the closed shops were now open.

How to describe Venice? Let's see, there are beautiful buildings in various pastel colors, such as lovely shades of blues, pinks, yellow and various shades of white, all with the ancient Roman/Greek architecture. The boys' description? "It's all old, run down and faded." So there you have it: two descriptions of the same place. There is water everywhere, instead of streets.

To get around you have to take a water taxi, water bus or a gondola. Our plan was to go to Florence next, but with the heavy traffic and it being an Italian holiday (we had just found that out), we voted to go north, closer toward home.

* * *

Then we headed into the mountains. The scenery was beautiful, but traffic was at a crawl. We slowly drove past vineyards and had an amazing view of the Southern Alps. We looked at our map and stopped at the biggest dot on the map to sleep over. We thought the bigger the dot the bigger the city; that is how we stumbled upon a city called Bolzano. It was late and we chose a hotel and settled in for the night. Our hotel had a Germanic style, with heavy wooden doors. It looked like it came straight out of Hansel and Gretel.

We knocked on the door while wondering if the building was really a pub. But it turned out to be a hotel with a pub. The hotel was something like an upscale cabin, but without the forest surroundings. It was very simple but beautiful, with plenty of indoor plants.

The next day was bright and sunny. It was really lovely in Bolzano, Italy. There is no other way to describe Italy. I had never heard of Bolzano but it's beautiful. It sits in the valley of the Southern Alps.

The interesting part about Bolzano is that some of the houses sit so far up in the mountains and you can't see a road that leads up to them. We wondered how people reached the homes.

The languages spoken were Italian, German, and Austrian; not much English. Bolzano is high in the Dolomite Mountains. I guessed they are special but I had to research that information. I discovered that Dolomites were named after a French mineralogist who discovered the rocks. Bolzano has castles and is noted as a popular ski resort town. Bolzano just may be the best kept secret in Italy.

After a nice breakfast of yogurt, coffee and pastries—Europeans

Art held little interest for the boys, but much of it was impressive.

eat a light breakfast—Cherri and I went shopping. Vincent discovered the shops earlier, and told us that some of them opened at 7 a.m.

Our hotel was located on a nice shopping street and one street over there was an ocean of shops. Bolzano has fantastic antique shops and plenty of boutiques, an outdoor market and more.

Bolzano could give Venice a run for its money as far as shopping goes, well, actually as far as beauty goes also. One has water and the other has mountains. There were shops in every direction.

We walked up hills, down hills and even went underground through a tunnel with shops built into the sides of the tunnel walls. Vincent took care of the boys and I don't know what they did. We communicated with walkie-talkies. When it was time to move on Cherri and I walked back to the hotel, our designated meeting spot.

Vincent called: "They saw a Lego set that they wanted and should I buy it for them?" he asked.

"I'll buy the Lego set since they were good while we shopped,"

The mountains of Northern Italy were breath-taking.

Cherri said. We walked back to the toy store. It was around noon. The shop was dark and the door locked. The shop owner let us in and said "It's time for break." The Kwapong boys were the last customers because she told the other people that came after us that the shop was closed and would open again in a few hours. The boys picked out a Lego soccer set.

"Aunt Cherri can shop all day," Kofi said, once the boys got their gifts. "Aunt Cherri can shop as long as she wants." This gave Cherri another 30 minutes of shopping. It's amazing what a set would get you. So, we went back to a shop where she saw a handbag earlier and she bought it. She likes unique things. Cherri looked in the window of a hardware store at door pulls. This was my last straw because the hardware store was closed and who looks at hardware on an Italy vacation? As she peered into the store window she discussed how nice the handle pulls were and how they would look on her kitchen cabinets.

"Dude, it doesn't matter, the store is closed," I said. Now that's a

Even high in the mountains, the boys found ways to play.

shopper for you. I was watching Oprah one day and interior designer Nate Berkus was talking about pulls and knobs he found in Greece. I guess there are more people like that than I thought. All was forgiven with the boys ever since she bought them that Lego set. Vincent was too polite to say anything, but he was as stunned as I was at her shopping talent. We walked back to the hotel with no complaints from the boys, met Vincent, loaded up the car, and drove for home.

I was hoping that we could start our drive home early to avoid too much night driving, but Vincent and the boys had other plans. For some strange reason unknown to man, they wanted to go to a park. Vincent's theory was that if they ran around they would fall asleep on the way home. We drove through the town of Bolzano and found a park after 15 minutes. The boys played while we enjoyed the view of the mountains.

The drive home was long, to say the least. We stopped for lunch somewhere in Germany. That was fine, but Vincent wanted to stop at a MediaMart store. For what? I guessed he figured Cherri looked in every store on planet Earth, so now it was his turn to get his fix.

The boys found another park close to Bolzano.

Vincent's drug of choice is electronics. Anyway, this took a good hour and a half out of our schedule. He bought the boys a camera. Couldn't that have waited until we reached the Netherlands, since our trip was over? Vincent was driving but I knew he would soon get tired. And he did. We got lost somewhere in Germany.

No one bothered to try and find out where we were. The road had a detour and the GPS couldn't pick up an alternative route. It was dark and late. Everyone was asleep but Vincent and me. Worse, we were the only stick-shift drivers in the car. All the signs were in German, as they should have been since we were in Germany. So, who does one ask for directions when everything was closed?

"I have to close my eyes for a minute," Vincent said, and pulled into a truck stop. I hadn't driven earlier because I was angry about his having taken too long in the store, but I changed my anger to common sense and drove the last three hours. I didn't think we should sleep in a car in a foreign country at a truck stop and not speak the language with three boys and a sister. I wanted to go home, not sleep on the side of the road at a truck stop. After hours of driving I finally saw a sign for the Netherlands.

We were way off track, I could tell because we came into the Netherlands from the south and we lived in the north. I could see fog on a lake and the sun just beginning to rise. We arrived home at about 4 a.m. I made a plate of poffertjes (mini puffed pancakes) for the boys. The boys stayed up as if it were Christmas morning and played with their new Lego soccer set. The adults went to bed.

June 2006: World Cup

Cherri had to borrow two big suitcases because the ones she brought with her were too small to fit all the stuff she bought from shopping. This happened in Ghana a few years back; she had enough art to start her own African museum of modern art. But that's another story. Vincent told me to tell her to put it in two suitcases; he didn't think it would pass the weight limit in one big suitcase. Before the train was scheduled to leave we had a good one and a half hours to shop. I took her to one of my favorite stores in Assen. And yeah, she brought something from there. She crammed it in her suitcase at the train station. She boarded the train to Schiphol Airport by herself with two big suitcases. I don't know how she handled this, because we were having a hard time getting her on the train, with just me and her.

* * *

In all the excitement of Cherri's visit and our trip, I missed a party invitation for Kofi. I hadn't checked my e-mail in weeks and I hadn't checked his school bag since we went on holiday. Kofi whined and grumbled. I told him we could make up for it by inviting Molly over for a play date. That always works when I forget a party. He stopped moaning after that.

Our evenings were filled with family soccer matches. Ato and Kwesi always picked Vincent for their team. Kofi said, "I'll take her." I was always picked last, just like in elementary school. I played goalkeeper, Kofi scored every point, played midfielder and was a fierce defender all at the same time. He would even take my place as goalkeeper and dive for the ball when the other boys had a free kick. I never dove for the ball. Maybe, just maybe, if I dove for the ball I would get in shape.

The weather was finally hot! I had been feeling low during the last two days. I needed a new exercise plan. We played soccer every evening. I was a bit surprised about my flabbiness because I rode my bike all the time. So it was back to jogging, I knew that worked.

The boys returned their plastic bottles to the grocery store. They collected 6.25 euros to share among the three of them. We watched three World Cup games—can you believe it? I don't even watch soccer unless Kofi is playing. I was eager for school to end and for us to return to the States (since I had to go back anyway).

On Sunday, Vincent and I went jogging. Well, we went walking. I told him I jog/walk. He looked at me with that "you're crazy" look and asked, "What is jog/walk?" I told him I jog and when I get tired I walk and when I get my energy back, I jog. We ended up walking. A quarter of the way into the walk, he wanted to turn around, he said his legs were itching. He said it happened when he jogged or walked but not when he played soccer. I walked him back home and then continued my walk/jog the way I wanted to in the first place. That took some bravery on my part, because if I saw a dog I would freeze. I was determined to face the dogs. To my surprise there was only one very small dog jogging with his owner. No panic there.

Kofi's soccer club had a family day at the field. I had to push the Kwapong boys to go. Kofi wanted to go over to our neighbor's house to play with his PlayStation game that only worked on a European system. It was hot again, too hot now. We went to family day and the Kwapong boys played on the bounce ride. Kofi rode the swing ride.

"Kofi is bored," Ato said.

"How do you know?" I asked him.

"Just look at him," he said.

After that, we played volleyball. None of us could hit the ball back to the other side. Everyone was dressed in orange, in support of the Netherland's soccer team, except us. We stuck out like sore thumbs. We were used to being the only black people at events outside of school, now we were also the only non-orange people as well.

The wheel on Vincent's bike was broken, so he wanted to drive to town to see if a bike shop was open. I didn't think a bike shop would be open on a Sunday. And of course the whole town of Assen was closed. Assen was very quiet, more quiet than usual, on a Sunday afternoon. The two younger boys fell asleep. We watched the World Cup again. This time Holland won 1-0. Kofi wanted England to win. I asked him why, since we live in the Netherlands.

"We live in Florida," he said.

I watched more soccer matches that weekend than I watched in my entire life. We watched a total of six games. The boys stayed up late to watch.

* * *

On Wednesday, Kwesi went on a play date after school with one of his mates. It was about a 25-minute drive and I was low on gas. I stopped at the gas station and ask the cashier to check and see if my bank card worked and if I could pay first and then pump gas. He said it worked and I had to pump the gas first. Which I did, then I found out the card needed a PIN number, which I didn't know—Vincent gave me the card without the number.

I told the cashier that I would go to the bank machine and get the money out, He told me to leave the car.

"I have kids in the car."

"Can't they walk with you?" he asked.

The bank was two buildings over and I could see the car with the two little ones inside it. The money machine said I had 80 euros in it but it didn't let me take the money out. I walked back to the gas station and told the cashier that the bank card was not working. He told me to fill out a form that specified that I had to pay him within 48 hours. I filled out the form. My address and license plate was all the information he needed. We drove to pick up Kwesi from his play date and stayed awhile. I had coffee and the other two boys played as well.

* * *

Thursday it looked like rain, but I rode my bike anyway. It was getting close to our moving date and the stress was building up. Going home should have been a piece of cake. I went to the bank to let them know my bank card was not working. The bank employee told me there wasn't money in the account. I told her yesterday the balance read 80 euros.

"That's not possible," she said (favorite Dutch words). "The money was transferred into the account a day ago but it takes the machine 24 hours to receive this information."

I tried my card at the bank. The card worked with plenty of euros in it, thanks to Vincent, who had deposited the money from Florida, where he was working. I rode my bike back to the gas station to pay for the gas from yesterday and there was a service charge of three euros for the paper work.

Everything costs. I received my first speeding ticket and couldn't remember when it happened. They sent the bill to the rental car company and the rental car company charged 11 euros for their paper work. The actual ticket was about 39 euros and I had to pay each bill separately. I would get a separate bill in the mail from the traffic court.

We watched part of Brazil vs. Japan. Ato and Kofi fell asleep early. Yeah! So Kwesi and I went to bed early. We all wanted Brazil to win because of Kofi's favorite player, Ronaldinho.

The cloudy weather continued through TT Assen weekend, which was a major motor bike competition. There also was a carnival in town with lots of vendors. The traffic was backed up. The moving man was late arriving due to traffic. When he arrived we went over everything that needed to be packed and shipped. We didn't have a lot to move. The furniture was rented. He said my Senseo coffee pot could not be shipped because it wouldn't work due to the different voltage. I loved my blue and green coffee pot.

* * *

The next week, a luncheon was held at Ponderosa for all the people leaving the British School. It was a lovely event. The food was buffet-style and quite good. There was a really nice rice dish made with coconut, I think. The chicken had a tasty peanut sauce. It was raining, but not the worst day. I finally learned how to bank on the Internet at the bank. The bank employee invited me into a private room and showed me step by step how to pay a bill. Coffee was in the lobby.

Ghana lost against Brazil during a World Cup match.

Ato and Kofi's farewell party was held with two other parents from Year 3. Ato's party was fairly cheap because the cost was divided among three parents, but Kofi's was funded by me, as there were no other children in Year 1 leaving. Tami added her younger son Sergei's Class F1 to Ivan's party so I couldn't leave Kofi out.

I watched Oprah the other day and psychotherapist Dr. Robin Smith asked the panel of guests at what age did they began to feel unworthy? I didn't want the boys to feel unworthy. According to the show, it lead to a woman overeating, another not eating and one feeling like trash. So all of the boys got a farewell party.

I worked on Kwesi's party later. He wanted a laser tag farewell party, but that was so out of the budget. Besides, he would be going to England for five days. Ato wanted a party at home instead of Ballorig; I called Tami to cancel our part of the deal, but when I asked Ato why he wanted a party at home, he said "So I can play PlayStation." I quickly called Tami back and arranged the party with her at Ballorig. Kofi didn't care, he just wanted a party. Then Ato wanted to know if he would get gifts. Kids today. So the party was planned carefully by Tami. The party would have been easy, but there were a lot of stragglers (uninvited siblings who were dropped off by their parents). I am a recovering straggler myself—I know what it's like to have one kid invited to a party and the others left looking sad and lonely—but I always stayed at the party to help out and would ask in advance if it was OK to bring extra kids.

The parents added the extra kids to the party as it was starting. We told the parents with the uninvited children to pay the eight or nine euros for them to stay, so our cost would be the same as planned. But we had to watch about ten extra kids, which wasn't easy. We needed more parents for the climbing wall. The parents had to help the employee running the climbing wall. The kids would make each other fall off the wall when no one was looking. That wasn't good.

Tami was busy with the four smaller kids. We had a total of four parents helping and that still wasn't enough. One parent thought it meant tug-of-war when we asked if she could help out with the climbing wall rope.

"Why didn't I get a going away gift?" Kofi asked his Year 1 class parent. She told him he would get a gift later. When the lunch came, a few kids' orders got mixed up because the parent handling the food didn't know we had a pre-arranged list. She was helping as best she could. I went outside with a group of kids who wanted to play in the warm weather. Kofi fell off the swings and cried himself to sleep. I woke him up when it was time to cut the cake. The cake from Ballorig tasted so fresh and good. Kofi just wanted the candy on top of the cake. Ato received presents from his Year 3 classmates and parents. All in all, the party was a success.

Kwesi spent the day at Donnie's. This was helpful because he was getting too old for kiddie parties. Plus this would have been one more age group to chaperone.

Later in the week, Kwesi was invited to a birthday/swimming party. Kofi was at a play date. Ato fell asleep on the way home from school and wasn't able to complain about not going on a play date. Believe it or not, the weather was great for a swimming party.

We were expecting a guest that afternoon. I didn't know the person, so I just had to see how it would go.

The school held its sports day at a nearby Dutch elementary school with a beautiful gym. The colors inside the gym were sky blue, red, and yellow. The design on the floor was artistic as well as functional. The teams were divided into three colors: green, blue, and red. Each color represented a province in the Netherlands. My boys were on the blue team, which was Friesland. The boys were all athletic. Kofi jumped the farthest in his group, so far that he almost knocked himself out. Kofi cried when he fell on his chin. I thought I would have to carry my baby out on a stretcher, the way they did in the World Cup, but he recovered quickly.

The audience was made up of parents who were really quiet. They didn't shout stuff out to their children the way Americans did at a kids' sport event. At the relay I did scream, "Go, Ato." He ran so fast that in the video of him running, he was in the frame all by himself, that's how far ahead he was of the other two teams. The green team had the most points at the end of the day.

Vincent even came to watch the first half of the competition. A few foreign parents told me at the end of sports day that the Americans had an advantage when it came to basketball. I told the foreign parents they had an advantage in the World Cup, but that in eight years Kofi would change the way the U.S. team played.

On Friday afternoon, Vincent picked up "Mystery Guest" from the train station. The man worked for the same company as Vincent in Miami. He was in Europe to attend the World Cup games in Germany and had stopped by the Netherlands for a visit. That was all we knew about him.

Mystery Guest was handsome, young, and strong. I told him that the only house rule was I didn't cook. So we drove to downtown Assen, I didn't know what else to do with him. I had to take Kwesi's bike to the repair shop and he rode with me.

The repair shop couldn't take the bike until next Thursday because it was their busy season. They were able to take Vincent's bike wheel. We walked a bit downtown. Our time was limited because our guest wanted to be back at the house in time for the start of the World Cup games. We went to the local Chinese restaurant and ordered take-out. We made it back within minutes before the start of the games. He wore his World Cup sports clothes for the team he wanted to win. He even had a matching team cap. He was so into the game on TV. The team he wanted to win won.

* * *

On Saturday our guest put on shorts (beautiful legs) and played soccer outside with the boys. Kofi and Ato really enjoyed his company. He began to sweat. "How come I don't sweat like that when I play soccer with the boys?" I asked.

Kwesi had a laser tag party to go to in Groningen. I asked Mystery (that's what I called him, because we didn't have a clue who he was) if he wanted to go into Groningen while we waited for Kwesi's party to end. We could go to a museum, shop or whatever and have lunch.

"Will you be back by 5 o'clock?" he asked.

I wouldn't, because the party ended at 5. Mystery didn't want to miss any of the World Cup, so he decided to stay home by himself. Vincent wanted to know why he had to go to Groningen with me. I didn't know my way around. Then Vincent wanted to know why I couldn't stay home while he took Kwesi. I might have wanted to play soccer with Mystery Guest, I joked.

The truth was, I had already called Nate and Thelma to meet us for lunch. I haven't talked to our American friends in weeks (I lost all their information on my million-dollar cell phone). They just happened to be in Groningen getting Nate a haircut. So that's what we did. We dropped Kwesi off and met Nate and Thelma for lunch.

I asked a parent to take Kwesi back to Assen when he picked up his son from the party. But by the time we were ready to leave the restaurant, it was close to 5 p.m. We waited at the laser tag party and bought Kwesi home ourselves.

Mystery had changed into a different team's jersey and was watching TV. Everyone played soccer between World Cup matches. The teams were Mystery, Kofi and me against Vincent, Ato and Kwesi. Kofi kept whining when the rules didn't go his way.

"Kofi is playing like he is scared, like Mom," Ato said. He did not want to be on Kwesi's team anymore since they were losing. We won by one point. Mystery's World Cup team lost.

"Every time I wear my Brazil shirt, they lose," he said.

Vincent and Mystery considered going into Groningen that evening to see the red-light district. I told Mystery he could see a prostitute in the morning after breakfast. It's a 24-hour operation in the Netherlands.

* * *

Another beautiful day. I signed us up for the bike event sponsored by the school, but instead we went on a field trip with the Smiths after their daughters attended a birthday party. We met them at our favorite spot, McDonald's.

"The Dutch must follow the manual the way the founders of McDonald's intended because everything is fresh," Nate said. "The bread is not soggy like in the States." Fast food in the Netherlands is not fast; they take their time and cook it as ordered instead of having the food warm under lights. After everyone chatted and had a bite to eat we went on a field trip to Giethoorn.

Giethoorn (goat's horn) is named because the people that settled the land found masses of goat horns, possibly dating from the 10th century (that's what I read). The settlers dug peat soil, mixed it, and spread it on the land to dry and then sold the peat to pay their taxes.

The long and short of this story is the villagers dug all around the houses creating lakes, canals, and ditches that were formed to transport the peat. They didn't dig the land with houses on them. These separate plots of land became little islands. There were about 10 or so houses on each island.

So, today you have a place known as "Venice of the North." You can only reach Giethoorn by boat. We parked our cars on the outskirts of Giethoorn.

We waited an hour to rent a boat large enough for ten Americans and a dog. Meanwhile, Vincent took a walk and found out that five minutes away we could have rented a boat without waiting. The houses had lovely gardens and thatched roofs. There were people in

The scene before our crazy boat entered the water.

motor boats, kayaks, and on a tour boat. Some people were in their bathing suits, enjoying this perfect day. We even saw someone in a bra (a bikini is a bra) but to actually see it was odd. All ten of us, including the dog, managed to fit into a large boat with a strong motor.

Mystery volunteered to be the boat's captain. Can one have a captain on a boat, or just on a ship? Vincent asked Mystery if he knew how to steer a boat. They reviewed the techniques and instructions given, which sounded simple. To go left, steer right. To go right, steer left. The catch was the captain sat in the back of the boat to steer. Well, well, well. Mystery crashed into several boats as we cruised along the canal. We rocked and crashed again and again.

The Dutch people started to stare, especially as we were approaching them. We began to stare at each other.

"I think we should switch drivers," Thelma said. She said this about five times. It got so bad that Ato started crying. That's when we decided to change drivers. This was not one of Mystery's strong characteristics. He should have stuck to soccer.

Setting sail for possible disaster.

Nate volunteered next. Even without Nate's eyeglasses, he was a far better captain than Mystery. Nate was singing the theme song to "Gilligan's Island." His confidence was so high that he suggested that we take the boat out to the North Sea. We stopped crashing, Ato stopped crying, and the Dutch people stopped staring.

We cruised along the canal for one hour exactly. The boat ride was only 14 euros. This was a really cheap family activity. One could keep the boat as long as one wanted for 14 euros an hour.

I wanted to look in the shops for a postcard. It was too late when we returned the boat, and the shops were closed. We decided to eat at a local restaurant in Giethoorn. We walked five minutes from the boat rental to the restaurant. After trying to seat ten people and a dog in the shade—the sun was hot—we put a couple of tables together and finally sat down.

We ordered ten drinks first. Vincent wanted to order right away but we didn't; that was our first mistake. The service was extremely slow, but we were not in a hurry. Order time: two orders of spare rib dinners (we looked on the plates of others), two orders of pancakes, three orders of Hawaiian tosti (one without ham and pineapples) and a potato salad.

We were all Americans, and used to a faster pace. But during our time in Europe, we all had grown to appreciate the slower pace and family atmosphere of the restaurants. So we were content to sit around, let Nate and Thelma's kid draw on napkins, and just enjoy the conversation as the courses of our meal slowly made their way to us.

* * *

On Monday, after dropping the boys off at school, I went home to clean the house. We had two weeks before moving day. The real estate agent and the Connect ladies came that morning for a "walk through" of the house to check for damages. The finish on the laminate floor was peeling off so I had to get that repaired before we moved. I wanted to ask about the walls with fingerprints, etc., but didn't want to bring up unnecessary repairs. They claimed we wouldn't be charged for normal wear and tear of living in the house—we would see. The house was sterile when we first moved in, so I wanted it to be sterile when we left.

I called the homeowners' father. He helped me when I needed information about the floor repairs. He said he would get someone to come take a look, but the man he sent didn't speak English. I decided to get my neighbor to help with the language barrier. I also had to change the light bulbs that blew out. The real estate agent asked "Didn't you use the oven; it's so clean?" I told you I didn't like to cook.

Mystery caught the train back to Germany that morning. He was a pleasant house guest. I didn't have any complaints about him. The boys wanted him to stay.

"Mr. Mystery is good," Ato said. "At least he's good at soccer."

* * *

Tuesday I went to a Delft store in Nieuw Buinen with Sharon and Carla. Sharon took the scenic route to Nieuw Buinen. Carla brought a map. Vincent had loaned out our GPS to his colleague.

China too good to eat from.

"Why would you loan out the GPS?" I asked.

"I didn't know you needed it," he said.

"I didn't know it was something I needed to say," I responded. So we went on a field trip the old-fashioned way, by paper map. Carla did a great job in getting us to Nieuw Buinen by map, after we drove through a few cornfields and back roads. Nieuw Buinen looked like a pretty suburban town. Once we got there, we stopped at the gas station and asked for direction to the Delft store. But the clerk didn't speak English. This threw me for a loop, because I had grown used to asking questions in English and getting answers. I did take Dutch lessons, remember. We found our way and enjoyed shopping in the Delft store. All three of us had big bags with our treasures and gifts for others. I stepped outside of my box and spend quite a bit of euros on a large soup tureen with the famous blue and white design Delft pottery is known for. Delftware goes back as far as the 16th century, and was copied from Chinese porcelain imports to keep the Dutch pottery makers from going out of business. That's how popular the

175

Chinese porcelain was in the Netherlands. It also speaks to a traditional Dutch policy of mercantilism, keeping business in the country instead of buying more imports than exports. We didn't go in the museum because we had to focus on shopping. You can't visit the Netherlands without bringing back Delft pottery.

Carla suggested that we visit Westerbork to see the Jewish memorial. It was a transportation place where Jews were held during the Nazi occupation of the Netherlands. We drove for what seemed like hours but we were pressed for time, we had to be back at school at 3:15. We were lost in the cornfields when I saw the sign to Groningen. I asked Carla if she knew the way, she said yes. We stopped and asked a Dutch man, his English wasn't great; but we thought he didn't understand us. Come to find out he was right. We should have taken his directions.

Carla had us in Westerborg, we wanted Westerbork. The "g" and "k" made all the difference in the world. We ran out of time and didn't get to visit the Jewish memorial.

* * *

End-of-year report cards were passed out. Why bother going to school the last seven days? On the front of the report was a space for children to write what they learned in school, a space for the Head Teacher to make his comments, and a space for the parents to write in their comments. Kofi's comment: "In Year 1, I learned to work the computer." Ato's comment: "I really liked this school because I did what I did last year and math was my favorite subject!" So in other words, he skated through that year because it was a repeat. The report card was an actual report with detailed paragraphs on your child's yearlong performance. Each subject was explained with great care. Kwesi didn't get his report, probably because he would be going to England soon with his class for the end of the year field trip.

Ato said, "Kofi got more A's because his class is easy, he should be in Year 2." Children repeat everything they hear.

Kwesi was packed for his trip. I gave him extra money to buy his brothers something at the sports store in England.

* * *

Sitting on a beach, waiting for a boat.

No other way to put it, it was as hot as you-know-where. We were miserable. One would think that coming from Florida would enable us to handle the heat, but no. Air conditioning was not common in the Netherlands. We had sweat beads forming on our foreheads at 6:45 p.m. and the sun was as hot as it was at noon. We began going to bed at midnight because it was so bright outside.

* * *

Ato's classmate had a leaving party at Hof van Saksen. Since Ato went to Kofi's classmate's party previously, Kofi got to go to Ato's classmate's party. That was the deal they made with each other. I told the boys that it was not their decision. One had to ask the parents of the classmates. The parents always said yes. Just when I thought I could have a few hours alone on the weekend, Kofi wanted to stay at the party. We tried to convince him to spend a day with Daddy, he didn't want to. So, I wound up at Hof van Saksen for three hours with a book. Another party for another child from the

177

The boys, as usual, made their own fun.

school was happening on the other side of Hof van Saksen It looked like half the school's student population was at this play place.

* * *

On Sunday, our day trip went sour. But it was our fault. The trip was to the Wadden Islands. Plan A: I got the boys ready; I packed lunch with fruit, sandwiches, and water. Vincent loaded the bikes. The weather looked bad, as if it would rain any minute, but we still decided to go because we only had six days left in the Netherlands. We didn't know the ferry schedule to the Islands. We chose to go to Schiermonnikoog. We drove through Groningen into Friesland. It was actually a lovely drive. The quaint villages and cows along the highway were typical Dutch scenery. Ato was not feeling well, he fell asleep in the back of the car. Kofi slept also.

We pulled up to the ferry dock. I asked the clerk when the ferry left for Schiermonnikoog; she said in 10 minutes. I asked if we could take the bikes; she said yes, for seven euros each. I went back to the car and told Vincent we had only 10 minutes to catch the ferry. He sent me back in to ask if we could walk. Someone had told Vincent that if we went early before the tides, we could walk across

the sea to the Island. When the tide is low you can actually walk across the seabed. The information woman said no, we couldn't. Yet we could see people out there, walking.

That left us with seven minutes to catch the ferry. We missed the ferry by one minute at most. The door was locked.

After talking to one of the workers (this is where it gets "Dutch") she told us that the next ferry arrived in four hours. OK. Plan B: The worker at the ferry told us that a half-hour drive would get us to another ferry. We drove through the lovely flat Friesland farm land. We got to the dock and had one whole hour to catch the ferry. We ate lunch. I ordered a coffee, the boys only wanted a drink, but I told them to eat something. So they ate the fries.

Vincent ordered lamb and fries. It must have been good, because Kofi ate it. Ato picked at his fries until he spilled his Coke on his fries and chicken fingers.

Vincent casually said, "We should go now." We got up to go and I suggested everyone go to the bathroom. Vincent removed the two bikes again. The boys and I waited in front of the dock until Vincent returned. He parked the car and came back. We went to get the tickets for the ferry ride and the clerk told us to go around the back with the bikes. We went around back with the tickets and the bikes. A man was locking the gate; he told us we couldn't get on the ferry, it was too late. The clerk could have told us to go through with our bikes instead of around the back, which caused us to miss the ferry. But rules are rules. That may be one of the biggest problems with the Dutch. The Dutch tend to be firm with their rules and way of life. Also, the Dutch don't give you the full information unless you ask; sometimes you don't know what to ask.

This was fine because we were late. I just couldn't believe that we missed two ferries. How was this possible? I am accountable for my action (I watched Dr. Phil and Oprah in the Netherlands). I respect the Dutch land and culture. I wasn't angry or sad. I felt like I was finally defeated by the Dutch.

While we were sitting on a dike in Friesland, Kwesi was traveling by ferry and train to England. He stayed in a log cabin (The Burrs Bunkhouse) in Manchester He canoed until he found out there were alligators in the lake. He bought Vincent a soccer jersey from Manchester United Stadium and met a professional soccer player. He did not call home the entire week. His roommate's mom told me the first night her son called because they locked themselves out of their room. He returned by airplane and said his end of year trip was great.

* * *

Finally, it was time to return to the United States. The train ride to Hamburg, Germany, was fast and furious; how we managed to get on and off three trains with six suitcases, three smaller bags, and three boys was also fast and furious. I hadn't expected the load of school papers each boy brought home. Their school papers could have been packed and shipped to the States. As any great mother knows, one has to keep the school papers as long as you can. I came across Kwesi's end of year comments. He said, "I have improved in math. I want to improve in literacy. I want to improve in art." I then realized how much work was accomplished during their year of schooling.

There was 10 minutes or less waiting time between each train. We had a system. I would jump off the train first with one boy and

Vincent would quickly pass the luggage to me and then he would jump off the train with the other two boys. We each grabbed a suitcase or two and walked as fast as we could to the next platform. How we knew which platform to go to and what train to catch was beyond me. I just followed Vincent and to my surprise he got it right every time. The system worked in reverse getting onto a train.

The weather was very warm, about 80 degrees, and the boys complained about the lack of air conditioning. We opened the windows.

The next day, Kwesi and Kofi wanted the usual McDonald's for breakfast. We walked them to McDonald's. I ate later at the hotel's executive room. Vincent's perks came in handy.

We caught two taxis to the dock. We checked in our luggage and waited in a long line to get on board. Once on board, WOW!!!! The *Queen Mary II* was stunning. It was about as British as one could get. It had an air of elegance, formality and tradition. We waved goodbye to Hamburg from the deck with the other passengers, and shortly afterwards set sail. After settling in our rooms, we ate a really nice Asian lunch. The boys couldn't wait to go to the children's room. We quickly learned our way to the Fun Zone with air hockey, foosball and the magic word of the day, X-Boxes.

We arrived in Southampton, England, on Monday. After we were told the train ride to London was one hour and 20 minutes, we decided to stay in Southampton. The boys weren't interested. Ato was already tired, Kwesi had just returned from London and Kofi said we could go to London another time.

Kofi was confident in our ability to finance travel at our leisure. We walked through a Toys R Us. The boys wanted to look around and see how much they had to save for something they wanted. We stopped at a huge sports store with a huge sale. The boys brought replicas of England's World Cup soccer jerseys. Ato's was a bit different. He said it was the goalie shirt. Who knew? We walked to a mall and when we returned to the ship, we saw a castle.

Soon we were at sea. On formal night, we dressed up and saw a show. Kofi slept through the entire performance. Vincent and Kofi went back to the cabin. I took Kwesi and Ato to the children's room. I began to feel dizzy, although I didn't feel the ship rocking.

* * *

On Thursday the sun came out. The ship seemed to move sideways. I grew wobbly. After breakfast Vincent took the boys to the Fun Zone and met me for Canyon Ranch's Pilates class. Pilates class was tough, and watching Vincent was funny. He would have made Mr. Pilates laugh.

Later I washed two loads of clothes. That wasn't my intent but better to play it safe than sorry. As we walked around the ship, Vincent was congratulated for his performance by other guests. He went out last night without me. I thought, "What goes on when I'm not around?" All day people walking by were smiling and saying "great job," congratulating Vincent. I found out later that there was an actor on board from the London Royal Academy of Dramatic Arts with the same skin tone as Vincent's. Other than that, there was no resemblance. Vincent went from being misidentified as a professional basketball player on the MSC *Opera* to being mistaken for a professional actor on the *Queen Mary II*. Being the kind gentleman that he was, Vincent merely smiled and took the compliments as if he had earned them.

Several guests on the ship asked me if Vincent was an author. Tyler Perry's picture was on the back of the book and one woman thought it was Vincent. He looks nothing like Tyler Perry. I was reading Tyler Perry's "Medea"—Don't make a black woman take off her earrings—you had to read the book to understand that.

I was surprised that the book was in the ship's fabulous library. I showed the book cover to rude Europeans when I ran into them. The rudest Europeans seemed to be the older ones. Some Europeans still wanted me to move out of their way and I refused. They would make a hissing sound or take a deep breath. After thinking about my tactics I decided to move out of their way for health reasons, if they were super elderly. I didn't think they could move if they wanted too. But then again, I met wonderful older Europeans and they made up for the nasty ones. I can't say they were all the same.

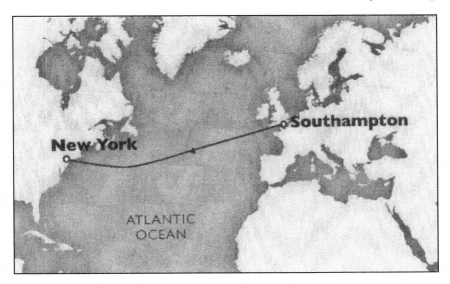

We went to the theater early to get good seats and were two rows back from the stage. We watched a comedy show that was so corny it was funny. Kofi laughed so hard, the couple sitting next to him said, "We enjoyed watching him laugh more than the show."

By Friday I was no longer sea sick. The dizziness passed.

I read "Medea's" section on child rearing to the boys every night and they loved it and laughed. Reading "Medea" to children may not be the best parenting advice. The boys took a long nap. They were alert and ready to go back to the Fun Zone. The Fun Zone closed at midnight. Vincent and I went to the club and got our groove back. We had a good time watching people dance.

Saturday was warm and brisk. We hadn't seen land for days. I could only imagine what a Tom Joyner cruise was like. The *Queen Mary II* was beautiful, wonderful, and spectacular. The guests were a bit dry, lifeless, stiff, and not much fun, unlike those on the MSC *Opera* who were very much alive and vibrant.

We found out that we were 55 miles from where the Titanic sank—as large as the Atlantic is, couldn't they have found a different route for us? Vincent and I earned certificates for attending at least three lectures of the Oxford Discovery Programme, taught by the University of Oxford.

Kwesi won a certificate from the Fun Zone for being the FIFA Soccer Champion; Ato made the best sun catcher, and Kofi was designated best air hockey player.

Our transatlantic crossing came to an end when we ran to the dock to see the Statue of Liberty as we headed for Brooklyn. After five days at sea we were ready to disembark. All went well.

We caught a taxi to the airport, then made our connecting flights to Florida.

Reflections

During my pregnancy with Kofi, my third son, I had a bout with breast cancer. I went through chemo while I was pregnant. I had to have Kofi by C-section. Later, I had more chemo as well as radiation treatment. Vincent had been offered a good position in North Carolina, and he was excited about the possibility. But as the cancer took hold, doctors and family members suggested that we stay put in Pittsburgh. Vincent agreed to put his ambition on hold for the sake of the family, so we stayed in my hometown. The experience would give me a better appreciation for my family, both the one I grew up with and the one Vincent and I created.

Their strength became my strength. Their sense of humor became my sense of humor. We would laugh, cry, and just enjoy being around each other. I learned that none of us can make it alone; we need family and friends in our lives to sustain us. Through my treatment and all that followed, I would often think about my grandmother down in Alabama who served as a source of inspiration for survival. My mother was a strong, elegant, and beautiful woman who taught us a positive work ethic, the importance of savings, and family solidarity. Through my treatment and all that followed, I relied on my family.

After Kofi was born, we had to uproot my family and move to Ann Arbor, Michigan, where Vincent had been accepted into the University of Michigan's MBA program.

I've been cancer-free for several years, and keep track of my progress by Kofi's birthday. It's ironic that a disease that can often be fatal brought new life into our family. And I praise God every time I think about how important family was to me in that time of crisis.

Little did I know how much that experience would prepare me for what came next.

When we moved to the Netherlands, the first thing that impressed me was the respect for families. The boys blended into Dutch culture with ease. The Dutch way of having special places for children to play helped keep the boys occupied. They made parents feel welcome by serving coffee while the kids played.

The boys depended on each other and always had each other as friends. I made a conscious decision to separate the boys, to allow each one to find his own identity and friends. I appreciated my family's flexibility in adapting to Dutch culture. Without effort on our part, we would have been isolated.

I was impressed with the Europeans efforts in socializing their children to get along with others. What helped break the ice was joining school groups, sports groups and having smart children, which is the right kind of popular.

I was pleased with the amount of education the boys received from the British School, even though all school year it seemed that they were not learning much because of the small amount of homework they received. Most improved were their reading skills.

I was delighted by our ability to participate fully in the culture and lifestyle of the Netherlands, instead of just going to school or work, coming home, and staying locked up in the house. Vincent's confidence allowed me to trust that he had a plan A, a plan B and a plan C if needed. I knew I was superwoman when I learned how to drive a stick-shift and would drive on European highways alone, not understanding the road signs and directions, and survive. I knew I was not superwoman when I was faced with protecting my boys from racism on the cruise ship, border crossing and occasional stares. However, I was determined not to let these incidents go without comment.

I wasn't ignorant about racism in Europe, and therefore it did not worry me before we went overseas. After all, I figured that I had experienced it enough in the United States to know how to handle racism if it emerged. But I wasn't quite prepared for the attitudes of Europeans who treated us better once they realized that we were not Muslims, as if being Muslim was a bad thing.

Cherri, in a letter she wrote soon after the trip, drew on her experiences as an education administrator in Pittsburgh to comment on the experience.

"Without a doubt, these trips have enriched me as a person," she wrote. "I learned things and experienced a part of life that I would never have been able to without the opportunity to visit my family during their stay. I know also that my three nephews gained tremendously from this experience, both socially and culturally.

"The educational gains were also apparent. As I visited their classrooms in Assen I saw the print-rich learning environment created through displays of student work. It was clear that cooperative learning took place, as student desks were arranged in small pods to foster sharing of ideas, information and group problem solving, all essential components—supported by research—to promote student learning."

Vincent brought an internationalist's point of view to our time in the Netherlands.

"Generally, at the site leadership level the Dutch worked as hard as what I was used to in the U.S., with family life getting the short end of the deal," Vincent said. "All other levels (mid to lower level employees) were more disciplined and stuck to a strong work-life balance, planning and taking extended holidays with their families."

The Dutch economy was thriving, unlike the States, where we're still fighting our way out of a recession. I learned that most Dutch people rent instead of purchase a home and live within their means. One of the biggest differences I noticed was the amount of stuff

Americans have and the amount of stuff you can actually live without. We had one TV in the Netherlands and got along fine.

When traveling with children, bring along their Legos, Game Boys, PSP 2 or whatever entertains them for long periods of time, even if it means you have to pack less to make room for their toys. Children will appreciate visiting children's museums because many of them in Europe offer hands-on exhibits. If you must skip the world-famous Louvre Museum in Paris for a lesser-known museum for the happiness of your smaller companions, just remember you're still in France, and what could be better?

Also, let them go to McDonald's if that's what they want (and I'm sure that's what they want). Almost every country we visited had a McDonald's. Give little people what they want to eat. It's not worth the hassle.

I knew that I needed one or two good native friends to help with everyday life such as grocery shopping, finding doctors, and interpreting Dutch into English. I was grateful to have met Martha and Gerta. Martha and I continue our friendship via e-mails; her daughter recently stayed at my home while vacationing in Florida.

Vincent remembers our year in the Netherlands as a legacy for Ato, Kwesi and Kofi.

"All in all it was a good experience," he said, "one that I would like to see my children carry on as they chart their own courses in life—not being afraid to explore new 'territories.'"

A year later when Cynthia visited me in Florida, she was shocked. "Wow, Lorene," she said. "I didn't know you had a house like this. Why were you so cheap in the Netherlands?"

That's when I learned what my American peers thought of me and my family when we first arrived in the Netherlands. They thought Vincent was mean, cheap and uncaring because we appeared to have few creature comforts (as Americans saw it).

They also thought that Vincent was making me do all the activities with the boys. They didn't know I participated because I enjoyed it.

Cynthia said she finally realized that we were different, conservative, and really in tune with our children. When the Americans I

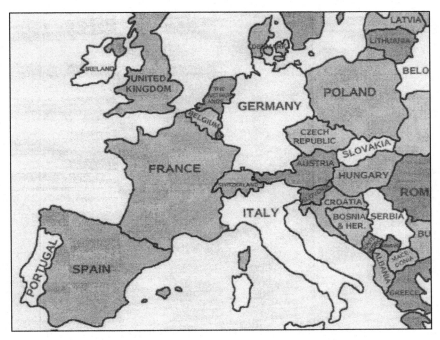

knew in the Netherlands understood my family better they appreciated that I chose to put my boys in all the activities; my family
would get in the car and take off, and I was my own woman. She
said, "You belong in the Netherlands."

From South Florida, USA, to the Netherlands is as different as
day and night. For one year I lived where families were the top pri-
ority. Children were happy and really wanted to go to school. Men
did not gawk at you. Young adults were not overworked. People
were not stressed out from spending long hours at work. Eating
fresh and healthy food daily was normal. Teenagers weren't sneaky.
The Dutch were not nearly as materialistic as the Americans. The
Dutch love their leisure time, families and nature more than money.
There is more to the Netherlands than marijuana, drugs, prostitutes,
and coffee.

Yes, I have to agree with Cynthia. I do belong in the Netherlands
and I am blessed to have had the opportunity to discover that!

Family Album

Venice, Italy

Travelling to new places is always accompanied by a sense of awe. To have the opportunity to experience different cultures is invaluable. For me, the European experience served as a paradigm shift as I learned from various artistic forms.

Kwesi

Athens, Greece

Keukenhof,
The Netherlands

From the modern functionalist Dutch styles to the Romanesque German architecture, Europe is a region with an intensely rich culture. It was these travels that inspired me to work to become an architect so that I too may possess artistic expression.

Kwesi

Athens, Greece

Groningen, The Netherlands

I remember LEGOLAND. Europe was fun. I would go again for a year and that would be fine. Four to six weeks would also be good.

Kofi

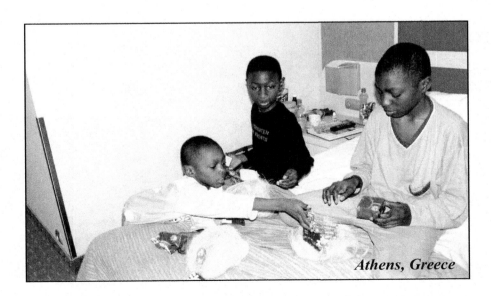

Athens, Greece

Assen
The Netherlands

School was nice. I enjoyed the small school. I found our house in the Netherlands more interesting with the steep steps and our house in the Netherlands had more places to hide when we played hide-n-seek. My favorite Dutch food is poffertjes.

Kofi

Assen
The Netherlands

Assen
The Netherlands

I enjoyed the snow.

I would go back to Europe again. I enjoyed the arcade room on our 18-day cruise. My favorite Dutch food is poffertjes.

Ato

Amsterdam,
The Netherlands

*Amsterdam
The Netherlands*

*Amsterdam,
The Netherlands*

Brussels,
Belgium

Roden
The Netherlands

Brussels, Belgium

Gadbjerg
Denmark

Hamburg,
Germany

Hamburg, Germany

Brussels, Belgium

Hamburg, Germany

Groningen,
The Netherlands

Bunne,
The Netherlands

Venice, Italy

Assen,
The Netherlands

At sea,
MSC Opera

St. Thomas,
USVI

**Basel,
Switzerland**

**Paris,
France**

Paris, France

Printed in Great Britain
by Amazon

83016735R00122